Seeing God Through The Storm

Empowering Truths from the Book of Job

Cover Photo by Reg Garner
http://reggarner.com/

Unless noted, all Scripture quotations in this book are (NIV) from the *The Holy Bible*, New International Version, ©1984 by International Bible Society

SEEING GOD THROUGH THE STORM Empowering Truths from the Book of Job
© Copyright 2013, ISBN 978-1-930547-81-0, Deeper Roots Publications
Orlando Florida 32818. Printed in the United States of America

All rights reserved. No part of this publication may be reproduced, stored in a retrieval system, or transmitted, in any form, or by any means, electronic, mechanical, photocopying, recording, or otherwise, without the prior written permission of the author and publisher.

Seeing God Through The Storm

Empowering Truths from the Book of Job

by
Joanna K. Harris

Deeper Roots Publications

Dedicated to:

*McKenzie, Sam, Nathan, Jan, Suzette, Rebecca,
Beth, David, Kati, Tracey, Anne,
and the rest of my E.I. friends.
I know you can relate better than most to Job's story.
Thank you for your friendship and prayers. You are precious to me!
As long as your storm continues to rage,
I pray you will continue to see more of your God.*

Table of Contents

Dear Reader……………………………………………………..…6
Introduction: Job's Storm……….….…………..…………….…7
1. Pleasing To God……………………………………….…..…9
2. The LORD……………………………………………….…14
3. Not My God………………………………………….……19
4. No Wrong……………………………………………….…23
5. Perspective……………………………………………….…27
6. Purpose………………………………………………….…31
7. No Fear……………………………………………….……35
8. Open Heart……………………………………………...…39
9. Heal Me……………………………………………….……43
10. No More……………………………………………….…48
11. Forgiven…………………………………………….….…52
12. God-Centered……………………………………….……57
13. Surrounded………………………………………….……61
14. God's Heart………………………………………….……66
15. Unlimited………………………………………….………70
16. God's Wisdom………………………………….…………74
17. Intimacy……………………………………….……….…79
18. For Me………………………………………..……………84
19. True Justice………………………………….…….………88
20. Brokenness……………………………………..….………93
21. Hope……………………………………………….………98
22. Faith………………………………………………………103
23. Glory And Honor………………………………...………107
24. Most Valuable……………………………………….……112
25. Motivation………………………………………….……116
26. God Speaks…………………………………………….…120
27. Look Around………………………………………..……125
28. Tremble…………………………………………...………130
29. Grace………………………………………………..……134
30. Restoration……………………………………….………140
31. Legacy………………………………………………….…145
Final Thoughts………………………………………….….…150
Discussion Guide………………………………………….…151
Acknowledgements……………………………………….…167

Dear Reader,

Storms are unavoidable in life; they will come. What a blessing to know we can walk through them with the God who rules over every storm. Whether you've known God for years or have just met Him, I pray through Job's story you'll come to know Him better.

Each chapter in this book focuses on a specific truth. While there is some overlapping of passages, the chapters mainly follow the progression of the book of Job. If you're able, I encourage you to read through the entire book of Job as you read this book. But if you can't, you'll still benefit from the Scripture portions quoted in each chapter.

At the end of every chapter are questions to help you think through and apply the truths in your own life. A journal page is also provided if you want to write out your answers to the questions, your thoughts, or your prayers to God. Journaling is a great tool and can be an encouragement to you later when you look back at what you've recorded.

There is also a Discussion Guide at the end of the book. You can use the discussion questions in a small group or one-on-one format for more in-depth study of the truths in each chapter.

May God bless you in your storm,

-Joanna

Introduction

Job's Storm

The book of Job is about someone who suffered the worst possible trial. Job lost everything—his wealth and possessions, his status, his friends, his children, and his health. Job had no one to comfort or encourage him, no Bible verses to cling to. He had nothing left but the air he breathed.

I've read Job's story many times. However, it was in the middle of an unrelenting health trial that this book of the Bible really came alive to me. In the midst of my own suffering, I could relate to Job's anguish. I could feel his despair. I could hear his pleas. I wept with him, and my heart echoed his cries for relief, for mercy, for God to do something!

Of the many trials I've experienced, some felt like a brief thunderstorm. Others were more like a category-five hurricane. In comparison, Job's "storm" was off the charts! In some of my trials, I could see the good things God was accomplishing. But Job couldn't. He didn't have Romans 8:28. (*And we know that in all things God works for the good of those who love Him, who have been called according to His purpose.*) Job couldn't see that there would be an end to his trial. He didn't know there would be a book written about him that would encourage millions of people over thousands of years. All Job knew was his intense suffering.

We don't know how long Job's trial went on, but before it was over, he made this significant statement to God: *My ears had heard of you but now my eyes have seen you* (Job 42:5).

At that point in the story, Job had gotten nothing out of his trial—no explanation, no apologies, no vision of future greatness—nothing. But he did receive one gift that changed him forever: Job moved from only "hearing" about God to "seeing" Him. Job saw God in his storm.

Isn't this what God desires for us in every hardship—that we would see Him? As we seek to know God better, to believe what is true despite how we feel, and to trust Him when nothing makes sense, we can learn to see God in our storms. We can discover more about who He is. We can understand more of His heart. We can know that experiencing a deeper friendship with Him is what makes every storm worthwhile.

The book of Job is full of thought-provoking questions, powerful emotions, and profound insights. Most of all, it contains empowering truths that can help us in this process of seeing God.

Whatever storm you're going through, be encouraged that with God there is hope and help. God wants to use the storms in our lives to draw us into a deeper intimacy with Himself. Join me on this journey of exploring Job's story, so together we can learn to see God through the storm.

Chapter 1

Pleasing To God

As a senior in high school, I was adjusting to a new town, new school, and new church youth group. Then halfway through the semester, my health collapsed. I had to quit school and youth group. I saw numerous doctors and spent months lying on the couch with barely enough strength to breathe. I felt scared, confused, and frustrated. I questioned God. "Why is my life being turned upside down? Why do I have to go through this suffering?"

Have you ever felt that way? Have you questioned God about a storm in your life? Have you wondered, "Did I do something wrong, God? Are you mad at me? Is this some kind of punishment?"

Being tossed around by a storm can make us feel like God is upset with us, mocking us, or out to get us. Nothing could be further from the truth, as the story of Job demonstrates.

> *In the land of Uz there lived a man whose name was Job. This man was blameless and upright; he feared God and shunned evil. He had seven sons and three daughters, and he owned seven thousand sheep, three thousand camels, five hundred yoke of oxen and five hundred donkeys, and had a large number of servants. He was the greatest man among all the people of the East.*
> -Job 1:1-3

Notice the Bible says Job was *blameless and upright; he feared God and shunned evil.* Job was a great and godly man, and everyone around him knew it.

> *One day the angels came to present themselves before the LORD, and Satan also came with them. The LORD said to Satan, "Where have you come from?"*

> *Satan answered the LORD, "From roaming through the earth*
> *and going back and forth in it."*
>
> *Then the LORD said to Satan, "Have you considered my servant Job? There is no one on earth like him; he is blameless and upright, a man who fears God and shuns evil."*
>
> *"Does Job fear God for nothing?" Satan replied. "Have you not put a hedge around him and his household and everything he has? You have blessed the work of his hands, so that his flocks and herds are spread throughout the land. But stretch out your hand and strike everything he has, and he will surely curse you to your face."*
>
> *The LORD said to Satan, "Very well, then, everything he has*
> *is in your hands, but on the man himself do not lay a finger."*
> *Then Satan went out from the presence of the LORD.*
>
> -Job 1:6-12

Are you surprised by what God said to Satan? God was so pleased with Job that He pointed him out to the enemy. *Have you considered my servant Job? There is no one on earth like him* (Job 1:8). Satan only scoffed at God. He challenged the Lord to strike Job's life and then see if he would still be godly. And God essentially said, "Okay, go ahead."

Can you imagine this? God purposefully allowed a serious testing in Job's life—because he was such a godly man, because God was pleased with him.

When storms come, the first thought we as Christians must embrace is that **we are pleasing to God**. Trials, hardships, persecution, suffering—none of these changes the fact that God loves us and is pleased with us.

How can we know that God is pleased with us?

Because of Jesus!

Jesus loved us so much that He came to earth as both God and man. Jesus lived a perfect life; then He took the punishment for our sin as He died on the cross. He conquered death by rising from the grave. When we admit our own sinfulness and trust in Jesus, we receive God's gift of forgiveness and eternal life. From that moment on, God says we are clothed with Jesus' own perfect righteousness (2 Cor. 5:21, Gal. 3:27). That's the way God sees us now and for eternity. Job was pleasing to God because of his blameless life of faith. How much more pleasing are we now that we have received the gift of Jesus' righteousness (Rom. 3:22, Phil. 3:9)!

It's true that our behavior isn't always pleasing to God. When we sin, it grieves God, because He loves us and He knows how sin damages us. In spite of the fact that we still sin, we are now completely wrapped in the righteousness of Christ. Colossians 3:3 says, *your life is now hidden with Christ in God*. There's no doubt about it, because of Jesus we are always pleasing to God.

> **because of Jesus we are always pleasing to God**

With this truth in mind, we can see that storms come into our lives for different reasons—but not because God is angry with us.

- Sometimes our trials are a consequence of a sinful choice we've made.
- Sometimes they're part of God's loving discipline. Hebrews 12:6 says, *the Lord disciplines those He loves*.
- Sometimes we experience hardship because of the sins of others, but that doesn't mean God is unhappy with us. Jesus said, *blessed are those who are persecuted* (Matt. 5:10). We are blessed and loved by the Lord, even when we suffer unjustly.
- Sometimes, like Job and like Jesus, we encounter storms because we are pleasing to God.

The suffering that God allowed in Job's life was not a punishment. It was, in fact, a reward—though not the kind of reward most of us want.

During the months I was sick in my senior year, my mom constantly reminded me that God was not angry with me, that He loved me very much. Gradually I heard God's voice calling me to the reward of knowing Him better through my suffering. In the process, I learned that regardless of my circumstances, I am pleasing to God because of Jesus!

Whatever storm you're facing today, remember that in Jesus you are pleasing to

God. God had a good plan for Job, the man He loved and was pleased with. I know He also has a good plan for you—the one He loves and is pleased with.

> *Once you were alienated from God and were enemies in your minds because of your evil behavior. But now He has reconciled you by Christ's physical body through death to present you holy in His sight, without blemish and free from accusation—*
> -Colossians 1:21-22

Thinking It Through:

a) Have you already received God's gift of forgiveness and eternal life by trusting in Jesus? If not, please take a moment to consider it. You can make that decision right now. Just talk to God. In your own words, say something like this:
"God, I know I'm a sinner, and I deserve to be punished for my sins. But I believe that Jesus died in my place to take my punishment. I'm trusting in His righteousness, not my own, and I gladly receive your gift of forgiveness and eternal life. Thank you, Jesus!"

b) If you've already received God's gift of salvation through Jesus, spend some time right now thanking Him. Praise God for the fact that you are pleasing to Him because of Jesus!

Seeing God Through The Storm

Chapter 2
The LORD

Knowing that we are pleasing to God regardless of our circumstances is a great comfort in the storm. But when the wind is raging and the rain is pelting us, it's easy to be overcome by worries, doubts, and fears. Are we at Satan's mercy? Is God bigger than this storm? Job knew the answers to these questions.

After God and Satan finished their conversation about Job, Satan left God's presence fully prepared to assault this innocent, unsuspecting man.

The LORD said to Satan, "Very well, then, everything he has is in your hands, but on the man himself do not lay a finger." Then Satan went out from the presence of the LORD.

One day when Job's sons and daughters were feasting and drinking wine at the oldest brother's house, a messenger came to Job and said, "The oxen were plowing and the donkeys were grazing nearby, and the Sabeans attacked and carried them off. They put the servants to the sword, and I am the only one who has escaped to tell you!"

While he was still speaking, another messenger came and said, "The fire of God fell from the sky and burned up the sheep and the servants, and I am the only one who has escaped to tell you!"

While he was still speaking, another messenger came and said, "The Chaldeans formed three raiding parties and swept down on your camels and carried them off. They put the servants to the sword, and I am the only one who has escaped to tell you!"

While he was still speaking, yet another messenger came and said, "Your sons and daughters were feasting and drinking wine at the oldest brother's house, when suddenly

> *a mighty wind swept in from the desert and struck the four corners of the house. It collapsed on them and they are dead, and I am the only one who has escaped to tell you!"*
>
> -Job 1:12-19

Can you imagine yourself in Job's place? In one day he lost all his possessions and wealth, almost all his servants, and all of his children. Job had to know this was not a coincidence. Losing everything at the same time? What would you have thought? I probably would have cried, "Satan must be out to get me!"

Look at Job's response.

> *At this, Job got up and tore his robe and shaved his head. Then he fell to the ground in worship and said:*
>
> *"Naked I came from my mother's womb, and naked I will depart. The LORD gave and the LORD has taken away; may the name of the LORD be praised."*
>
> -Job 1:20-21

These verses amaze me! My little trials are nothing compared to what Job went through. Yet I tend to complain, get angry, or despair. Job had every reason to respond like that, but he didn't. Job expressed his grief over all he had lost, but then he **worshiped**. He didn't shout curses at the enemies who robbed him. He didn't even blame Satan for attacking him. No. He worshiped the LORD. He said, *The LORD gave and the LORD has taken away; may the name of the LORD be praised* (Job 1:21).

How could Job worship at a time like this? I think it's because Job acknowledged God as the LORD—"Yahweh."

Most English translations of the Bible use "LORD" for this Hebrew name of God that occurs throughout the Old Testament. The name "Yahweh" was sacred to the Jews. Today it's hard for us to comprehend the glorious significance of this name.

When Yahweh revealed Himself to Moses, He said, *I AM WHO I AM. This is what you are to say to the Israelites: "I AM has sent me to you"* (Ex. 3:14). There is no greater statement of God's character, power, and sovereignty than "I AM." Only Yahweh, the LORD, can say, "I AM," because He alone is the source of all things. All of the rest of us, including Satan, are created beings. God is the Creator. He holds all power and authority. Nothing in this universe happens outside of His control.

When we see "the LORD" in the Old Testament, it reminds us of these truths. Yahweh—the LORD—is the sovereign "I AM."

Job recognized this truth that is often hard for us to understand: the LORD is in control of everything. Every single thing! Yes, Satan carried out wicked deeds against Job, but he had to have God's permission first. That's why Job could say, *The LORD gave and the LORD has taken away* (Job 1:21). In spite of everything bad that happened to Job, miraculously he kept his focus on who God is. Job was able to worship because he acknowledged the LORD.

the LORD is in control of everything

What about you? Can you trust that the LORD is in control of your storm—that He has either allowed it or planned it to happen in your life? Maybe that's hard for you to accept right now. I understand. I've struggled with this truth as well.

I grew up as a missionary kid in Colombia, South America. That is, until Communist guerrillas swarmed our school base and kidnapped two of our missionaries. We were forced to evacuate. Our lives were disrupted, the missionary efforts were hindered, and the families of the kidnapped men were forever changed. Where was God? Were we victims of evil men? Were we at Satan's mercy?

Months later God answered my questions by showing me that He was in control of every detail. As I replayed that day in my mind, I saw His hand clearly. Yes, He allowed evil men to disrupt our lives, but they couldn't destroy us. From that experience I realized that God is indeed sovereign.

I believe that God's sovereignty is the security we need in uncertain times. It's the truth that sets us free from worry, fear, and guilt. God's sovereignty means we aren't at the mercy of sinful, wicked people who harm us. They can only do what God permits. It means we aren't held captive by Satan's attacks. He, too, must submit to God. It means we aren't doomed to constantly blame ourselves or carry guilt for wrong decisions. God allows us to make our own choices, but He forgives our sins and teaches us through our mistakes. Because God is in control, we know He will keep His promise to work all things for our good and for His glory (Rom. 8:28). His sovereignty covers every situation.

Whatever our circumstances, the knowledge of God's sovereignty is our anchor in the storm. We can know that God, the LORD, is ultimately in control of everything that happens in our lives. He is bigger than the storm!

Even in Job's excruciating trial, he was able to offer praise because he had confidence in the sovereignty of God. We can do the same. We are in the hands of the LORD. There's no better place to be.

Thinking It Through:

a) Do you believe that the LORD is in control of your storm right now? How does that make you feel?

b) Can you praise God that He is sovereign—that you aren't at the mercy of Satan, wicked people, or your own mistakes? Ask God to help you apply Job's prayer to your own situation. "Lord, you give and you take away. Blessed be your name."

Seeing God Through The Storm

Chapter 3

Not My God

More than a year after my family evacuated from Colombia, we got word that our two kidnapped missionaries had been killed. After all the months of hoping and praying for their release, this news was not what we expected to hear. If God is in control—and we know He is—why does He allow such things? What is He thinking? How can this make sense? Reading Job's story often leaves me with similar questions.

> *On another day the angels came to present themselves before the LORD, and Satan also came with them to present himself before Him. And the LORD said to Satan, "Where have you come from?" Satan answered the LORD, "From roaming through the earth and going back and forth in it."*
>
> *Then the LORD said to Satan, "Have you considered my servant Job? There is no one on earth like him; he is blameless and upright, a man who fears God and shuns evil. And he still maintains his integrity, though you incited me against him to ruin him without any reason."*
>
> *"Skin for skin!" Satan replied. "A man will give all he has for his own life. But stretch out your hand and strike his flesh and bones, and he will surely curse you to your face." The LORD said to Satan, "Very well, then, he is in your hands; but you must spare his life."*
>
> -Job 2:1-6

Job passed the first test well. He praised God for His sovereignty. Rather than applauding Job, God pointed him out to Satan a second time. Satan challenged God to allow him to strike Job once more, this time in Job's body. Again, God said, "Okay."

To me, verse six is probably the scariest verse in the whole book of Job. *The LORD said to Satan, "Very well, then, he is in your hands; but you must spare his life."* God said Job was in Satan's hands. Satan could do whatever he wanted to Job, except kill him. At first when I read this verse, I thought, "No way! That's not my God saying that!" I honestly couldn't imagine my loving, heavenly Father letting Satan do whatever he wanted with one of His precious children. How could that be?

As I pondered this dilemma, I heard a quiet answer: None of us knows God as well as we think we do.

This is an important theme in the book of Job. In the final chapter, Job told God, *My ears had heard of you but now my eyes have seen you* (Job 42:5). Before his trial, I imagine Job thought he knew God pretty well. By the end of the story, Job realized how much he still had to learn. Job's friends also thought they had all the answers, but God said they hadn't spoken what was right of Him (Job 42:7).

> **The LORD is more awesome than we can possibly imagine!**

When I say that we don't know God as well as we think we do, I don't mean He is in any way worse than we think He is. I mean He is MORE—greater, higher, larger, grander—than we think He is. In Isaiah 55:8-9 God said, *"For my thoughts are not your thoughts, neither are your ways my ways," declares the LORD. "As the heavens are higher than the earth, so are my ways higher than your ways and my thoughts than your thoughts."*

The LORD is the Creator God. We are His creation. Of course we can't fully grasp or understand all of who God is and what He does. If we could comprehend everything about Him, then He wouldn't be God. He would be limited like us. The very fact that we can't completely understand Him should encourage us. The LORD is more awesome than we can possibly imagine!

The miracle is that God wants us to know Him better. He wants to reveal more of Himself, His ways, and His heart. He doesn't want us to believe things about Him that aren't true. Sometimes it seems God goes to great lengths to make us question what we think we know about Him, so we'll seek to discover Him as He truly is.

Think back through your life. What have you learned about God during the easy times? What have you come to know about Him in the hard times?

God uses the storms in our lives to show us more about who He is—His mercy, kindness, faithfulness, love, and grace. Even when storms don't make sense to us, they are opportunities to expand our understanding of God.

As long as we live, there will always be more for us to learn about God. Some things, such as Job's experience and our beloved missionaries being martyred, may not be fully explained until we reach heaven. The question is, will we allow unexplained hardships to push us away from God or to motivate us to seek Him more?

When something happens that makes us say, "That's not my God!"—it's time for us to pause. It's time to acknowledge that God is bigger than we can imagine. It's time to look in God's Word for the truth about who He is. It's time to pray, "Lord, I want to know you better. Please show me more of yourself through this storm."

I know He will.

> *So I say to you: Ask and it will be given to you; seek and you will find; knock and the door will be opened to you. For everyone who asks receives; he who seeks finds; and to him who knocks, the door will be opened.*
> -Luke 11:9-10

Thinking It Through:

a) How well do you think you know God? How well do you want to know Him?

b) List some specific things you learned about God during a previous storm in your life. What is He revealing to you about Himself right now?

Seeing God Through The Storm

Chapter 4

No Wrong

Have you ever felt like your circumstances were so awful that things couldn't possibly get worse? Then they did. I've been there. It's not fun. Maybe that's how Job felt at the end of chapter one. His life had been devastated—but it was about to get even worse.

After God told Satan that Job was in his hands, Satan didn't waste any time.

> *So Satan went out from the presence of the LORD and afflicted Job with painful sores from the soles of his feet to the top of his head. Then Job took a piece of broken pottery and scraped himself with it as he sat among the ashes. His wife said to him, "Are you still holding on to your integrity? Curse God and die!" He replied, "You are talking like a foolish woman. Shall we accept good from God, and not trouble?"*
>
> -Job 2:7-10a

Not only was Job in physical agony, but his wife turned against him as well. Even then Job honored God by acknowledging His sovereignty and accepting this new affliction. *In all this, Job did not sin in what he said* (Job 2:10b). More specifically, *Job did not sin by charging God with wrongdoing* (Job 1:22).

When I've encountered storms, my first reaction has often been to question God. "Why me? Why this? Why now?" If I felt like God wasn't answering me, then I was tempted to blame Him. Negative thoughts crept in. "I don't deserve this. God, you could change this situation if you wanted to. You must not love me as much as you love other people."

Can you relate?

I've learned that at the heart of these negative thoughts and feelings is the simple belief that God is not good. We often reason that if He were good, He would give us an answer, change our circumstances, or make life easier for us. We tend to measure God's goodness by how we feel or by what is happening in our lives.

The Bible says Job did not sin by charging God with wrongdoing. Job had plenty of reasons to doubt God's goodness. But he didn't. Most of our trials are small in comparison to Job's, yet how often do we accuse God of doing something wrong? "God you made a mistake. You aren't being fair. You don't care." All these responses actually mean: "God, you must not be good."

We've learned that we don't know God as well as we think we do. However, if we don't know that God is good, perhaps we haven't begun to truly know Him.

If God is not good, then He is not truly God. By definition, He must be good. By evidence of creation and by what God says about Himself in the Bible, we know He is good. However, knowing and believing are at times worlds apart.

Throughout the Bible, God declared again and again the truth that He is good. *For the LORD is good and His love endures forever; His faithfulness continues through all generations* (Ps. 100:5). *Give thanks to the LORD, for He is good; His love endures forever* (Ps. 118:1). *I am the good shepherd; I know my sheep and my sheep know me* (John 10:14).

Believing that God is good is a step of faith each of us must choose for ourselves. If you haven't wrestled with this choice yet, you probably will at some point.

For many years I had no problem believing that God is good. But eventually a painful trial stripped away my shallow belief in God's goodness. I knew intellectually that God is good, but I couldn't accept it because of what I saw and felt. I couldn't explain the mystery of suffering in the world. I couldn't answer all my questions. I finally realized that I simply had to choose. Would I believe what God says—He is good—even though it doesn't always make sense to me? Or would I believe the lie—God is not good—which only leads to more misery? In His great mercy, God gave me the strength to choose to believe the truth.

God is good. He does no wrong.

I may not always understand what I see or experience, but I know God is bigger than my ability to understand. I may question or wonder why the LORD does what He does, but I know He's always good. He never makes a mistake, never messes up, never acts unkindly. He is constantly working out good plans and purposes that I can't begin to see. When I get to heaven and view everything from God's perspective, I know I'll not only understand, I'll be amazed at the goodness of my God!

I can't imagine how Job must have felt. First he lost everything, and then he endured physical torment. How could he answer his wife so calmly? In his suffering, Job didn't curse God. He didn't deny God. He didn't accuse God. Job held on to the truth that God is good—He does no wrong.

God is good. He does no wrong.

When life seems to get worse, and worse, and even worse, the truth of God's goodness is a lifeline for you and me. When we grab hold of this truth, no matter how fierce the storm, we can know it will guide us safely through the wind and the rain to our Refuge.

Thinking It Through:

a) Do you agree intellectually that God is good? What might hinder you from believing that He is good?

b) How have you experienced God's goodness in the past? How can believing that God is good help you in your storm today?

Seeing God Through The Storm

Chapter 5

Perspective

In my junior year of college I was diagnosed with rheumatoid arthritis. Every little movement became an ordeal for me. I couldn't brush my hair, climb stairs, or turn a doorknob without pain. Even though I was exhausted, I had difficulty sleeping. Pain medications helped somewhat, but left me feeling disconnected from the world. I struggled each day just to get out of bed.

In the middle of a storm like this, it's hard to see things clearly. Even when we know God is good, pain can blur our vision. Exhaustion can distort our perspective.

Amazingly, Job responded to his trial with worship and faith. He remembered God's sovereignty and goodness. At this point, God could have said, "Well done," and restored Job immediately. Isn't that what we'd expect? But God had a different plan. Job's trial had barely begun.

> *When Job's three friends, Eliphaz the Temanite, Bildad the Shuhite and Zophar the Naamathite, heard about all the troubles that had come upon him, they set out from their homes and met together by agreement to go and sympathize with him and comfort him. When they saw him from a distance, they could hardly recognize him; they began to weep aloud, and they tore their robes and sprinkled dust on their heads. Then they sat on the ground with him for seven days and seven nights. No one said a word to him, because they saw how great his suffering was.*
>
> -Job 2:11-13

Job's suffering went on so long that his friends heard about it and made a trip to visit him. When they arrived and saw Job, they were shocked. Apparently what they'd heard hadn't prepared them for the intensity of Job's anguish. The Bible says they didn't speak a word—they just sat with him for a whole week.

If even Job's friends were speechless at the sight of his suffering, how can we comprehend how horrible it was? Job literally lost everything, including his children. His wife told him to curse God and die (Job 2:9). Job's other friends deserted him, and people who once respected him mocked him (Job 30:1). Job had unrelenting pain and couldn't sleep because he was terrified by nightmares (Job 7:13-15). He said, *I am nothing but skin and bones; I have escaped with only the skin of my teeth* (Job 19:20).

Let's put things in perspective. You and I may be enduring storms right now, but we'll probably never suffer as much as Job did. And we have more advantages than Job. He didn't have the Bible. We have this awesome book full of God's promises, comfort, and encouragement. Job lived long before Jesus came to earth. Today we know God not only as the good and sovereign LORD but also as our sympathetic Savior, Jesus Christ (Heb. 4:15). Job didn't have the Holy Spirit living inside him as believers do today (John 14:16-17). Without all these precious gifts, it's remarkable that Job didn't abandon his faith.

> ***we have more advantages than Job***

When a painful storm strikes, how quickly do we forget all God has given us both materially and spiritually? Are we like Job's friends, who saw only the suffering? Or do we ask God to give us His perspective?

Changing our perspective doesn't mean we deny our pain or pretend everything is okay. It does mean we ask God to help us focus on something different:

- on what we have instead of what we lack,
- on who God is instead of how we feel,
- on what God has said instead of what we see.

Job didn't have all the blessings we have today, but he did have one very important thing—God's favor. God was watching over him and working out His plan because He loved Job. Job needed someone to help him see things from God's viewpoint. We need that too, especially in a storm.

During the months I suffered with arthritis, God was faithful to send me help and encouragement. He brought me through those terrible days. God eventually brought Job through his storm too. Can you believe the LORD will bring you through yours?

Thinking It Through:

a) For at least one minute, don't think about your suffering. Instead, make a list of the gifts and blessings you have that Job didn't have. Thank God for each item on your list.

b) What have you learned about God from the first two chapters of the book of Job? Ask God to keep changing your perspective to be more like His.

Seeing God Through The Storm

Chapter 6

Purpose

As the winds of your storm continue to blow, maybe you've had thoughts like, "Why was I born in the first place? My life is only pain. What's the point of my existence?" If you've thought this way, you're not alone.

After Job's friends sat with him in silence for a week, Job finally spoke. However, his words were no longer ones of worship.

After this, Job opened his mouth and cursed the day of his birth...
"Why did I not perish at birth, and die as I came from the womb?"
-Job 3:1, 11

After all Job had suffered, it's no surprise he felt like cursing something. His emotional loss and physical pain were so overwhelming that he wished he'd never been born.

I can understand why Job would feel that way. Can you? His pain made him forget all the ways God had worked through him and all the times he'd been a blessing to others. Only later did he recall some of the good things.

...I rescued the poor who cried for help, and the fatherless who had none to assist him. The man who was dying blessed me; I made the widow's heart sing... I chose the way for them and sat as their chief....
-Job 29:12-13, 25a

Job's life was important and valuable. Consider how many people would have suffered if he'd never been born. Imagine their pain if Job hadn't been there to help them. God created Job for a reason. In his agony, Job forgot that God had a purpose for his life.

When we're in anguish, it's hard to remember this truth. It's easy to let Satan feed us lies of discouragement and despair. Job spoke out of his pain.

Why is light given to those in misery, and life to the bitter of soul?
-Job 3:20

Why is life given to those in misery? Why can't we just die when life seems unbearable? Because God has a purpose for our lives!

We were created for both a general purpose and a specific purpose.

God created us for the general purpose of bringing Him glory, as He said in Isaiah 43:7, *everyone who is called by my name, whom I created for my glory, whom I formed and made.* We can fulfill this purpose regardless of our circumstances. God is glorified simply by our heart's response to Him. In each small offering of thanksgiving, praise, love, or trust, God is honored. Though no one else may notice, heaven rejoices, and God is glorified. Job probably had no idea that all of heaven was watching his response. By refusing to curse God, Job fulfilled His purpose of bringing glory to the LORD.

God also has a specific purpose for each of us, consisting of good deeds that we were created to do. *For we are God's workmanship, created in Christ Jesus to do good works, which God prepared in advance for us to do* (Eph. 2:10). The *good works* God has prepared for us can be as simple as praying for someone or as detailed as translating the Bible into another language. God shows us one step at a time the good things He has for us to do. When the path is dark, we shouldn't despair. We never know what significant thing God will do through us next.

In every storm, knowing that God has a purpose for us is a great encouragement. I experienced this truth vividly during my last semester of college. I was eagerly preparing to go to Mexico as a missionary. Then I was in a bad accident. My car was totaled, and an ambulance took me to the hospital. The EMT's deposited me in the hallway, filed their paperwork, and left. There I was on the gurney, flat on my back, my neck in a brace, staring at the ceiling. I didn't think I was seriously injured, but as the seconds ticked by, my fears and uncertainties pushed me to the edge of panic.

Suddenly a friendly face appeared above me. One of my friends had heard of my accident and rushed to the ER. She must have sensed my anxiety, because she smiled at me and said emphatically, "God's not done with you. You still have to go to Mexico!"

That was exactly what I needed to hear. In the midst of my fearful circumstances, my friend reminded me of God's purpose for me. This storm could not stop God's plan! As the nurse wheeled me away, I embraced that thought, and the panic subsided. Praise God, my injuries were minor, and I was able to return to classes a few days later.

No matter how severe the storm becomes, we must believe that our lives have purpose. Because God is sovereign, we know whatever storms He allows cannot erase His purpose for us. And sometimes we cannot experience His purpose unless we go through the storm. Remember Jesus' friend, Lazarus? He had to experience sickness—and even death—so Jesus could raise him from the dead (John 11). It was through that storm that God fulfilled His purpose for Lazarus. For the rest of his life, Lazarus was a walking reminder of the power of God and the truth that Jesus is the Savior.

God created you for a purpose. He put you on the earth, in this place, at this time, for a reason. God wants to do great things through your life. He probably already has. And though you may not realize it, your storm right now may be the very thing you need for God to accomplish His purpose for your life.

Whatever you're going through today, praise God for the day of your birth. And thank Him for His promise to fulfill His good purpose for you.

The LORD will fulfill His purpose for me; your love, O LORD, endures forever....
-Psalm 138:8

Thinking It Through:

a) List some ways you've seen God use your life to bless others. Next to each one, write: "God has a purpose for my life." Reread your list whenever you feel discouraged. Rejoice in what God has done and is doing through you.

b) Think about the people who have blessed your life the most. What trials have they experienced? What does that tell you about God's purpose for your own storm?

Seeing God Through The Storm

Chapter 7

No Fear

None of us would ever choose to experience storms. We know how easily the stress from a storm can overwhelm us. However, the stress we place on ourselves when we live with fear can be even more harmful.

After Job cursed the day of his birth and vented some of his emotions, he finished his speech by saying, *What I feared has come upon me; what I dreaded has happened to me. I have no peace, no quietness; I have no rest, but only turmoil* (Job 3:25-26).

It's not clear if Job had feared suffering in general or the specific trial of losing everything. But clearly he had feared something dreadful. It seems strange that a godly man like Job lived with fear. Yet I'm not much different. Are you?

When life is calm, we're often fearful of what might happen to us. And once a painful storm hits, fear can engulf us. The world doesn't feel safe; God doesn't seem trustworthy. Fear leaves us, as Job said, with *no peace, no quietness…only turmoil*.

What can we do when fear takes hold in our lives?

We can remember what we've learned from Job's story so far.

- God is in control,
- God is good,
- God has a purpose for us.

These truths are vital weapons for combating fear. But perhaps there's another truth we need even more than these.

> *There is no fear in love. But perfect love drives out fear….*
> -1 John 4:18

The best remedy for fear is a growing understanding of God's perfect love for us. Paul wrote in Romans 5:5 that *God has poured out His love into our hearts by the Holy*

Spirit, whom He has given us. God has given us the Holy Spirit to help us understand and experience the extraordinary love of God. We are loved by God; that's an eternal fact. Through God's Word and the work of the Holy Spirit in our hearts, we can grow in our knowledge of God's love for us personally (Eph. 3:17b-19).

The more we understand the love of God, the more we'll realize that everything the LORD allows in our lives is motivated by His love for us. As we grow in God's love, the fear will gradually be driven out. Fear cannot remain where love reigns.

And when the thing we feared does happen, as it did with Job, we have something Job didn't have. We have God's promise in Romans 8:28. *And we know that in all things God works for the good of those who love Him, who have been called according to His purpose.*

In all things, God works for our good—because He loves us and has a purpose for our lives. Just as it was for Job, our storm may be painful, it may be devastating, it may feel like we're being crushed. But out of it we'll experience the good God intends. That's the promise of His love.

During my first year as a missionary in Mexico, I became very ill. After six weeks with no improvement, I had to return to the States. Fears and questions abounded. What was I going to do? Would I get to go back? Why was this happening?

> **Fear cannot remain where love reigns**

In those difficult days, God reminded me of His love and helped me cling to His promise. About three months later, I was able to return to Mexico with a renewed enthusiasm for ministry

I know we don't always see the fulfillment of God's promise right away. Sometimes we can't imagine what possible good God will bring from our pain. But by faith we can choose to focus on what is true. We can declare out loud: "I know God loves me. I know He will be faithful to bring good from this. I believe His promise. I will rest in His love and not be afraid!"

Worry, dread, and fear always harm us. Fear never produces anything worthwhile;

it only causes inner turmoil. Thinking about God's love for us and dwelling on His promise in Romans 8:28 will drive out fear and restore our peace.

Is there something specific that you fear or dread, that you hope will never happen in your life? Whenever you feel the fear rising up inside, pause and consider God's great love for you. Remember His promise and boldly declare, "No fear!"

> *I sought the LORD, and He answered me; He delivered me from all my fears.*
> -Psalm 34:4

Thinking It Through:

a) What are you fearing or dreading right now? How does it make you feel?

b) How can God's promise in Romans 8:28 help you in your current storm?

Seeing God Through The Storm

Chapter 8

Open Heart

Have you ever received advice or unwanted counsel from someone who hasn't experienced the kind of storm you're going through? It's not a pleasant experience, is it? During my various health trials, some doctors told me, "It's all in your head." Other doctors suggested that I didn't really want to get well. Even a few Christian friends implied that if I confessed some sin or went to counseling, my health would improve. Usually people mean well, but they don't realize how their insensitive words can wound us.

I'd have expected Job's friends to offer sympathy and encouragement after seeing his intense suffering. That wasn't the case.

Eliphaz spoke first. He said, *now trouble comes to you, and you are discouraged; it strikes you, and you are dismayed* (Job 4:5).

Saying that Job had "trouble" was a ridiculous understatement. Eliphaz had the audacity to rebuke Job for being discouraged, though Eliphaz had obviously never faced suffering like Job's.

That wasn't all. Eliphaz continued, *Consider now: Who, being innocent, has ever perished? Where were the upright ever destroyed? As I have observed, those who plow evil and those who sow trouble reap it* (Job 4:7-8).

Eliphaz basically told Job, "You must have done some wicked thing to deserve this trouble." He went on, *But if it were I, I would appeal to God; I would lay my cause before Him* (Job 5:8). Yet, how could Eliphaz know what he would do in Job's situation? He was giving advice about something he'd never experienced. He finished his speech by saying, *We have examined this, and it is true. So hear it and apply it to yourself* (Job 5:27).

Eliphaz was confident, but that didn't mean he was right. He was, in fact, mistaken in his opinion that Job's suffering was a result of sin. Job 1:1 clearly states that Job was blameless. However, even though Eliphaz had a wrong opinion of Job, God could still bring something good from his speech. In Job 5:2 Eliphaz said, *Resentment kills a fool, and envy slays the simple.* He was right about that.

As we go through storms, there will be people who are insensitive, arrogant, or constantly giving advice. At times I've felt hurt or angry with such people. I've thought, "They don't live my life. They don't feel my pain. How can they tell me what to do?" If left unchecked, these kinds of thoughts and feelings can easily turn into an attitude of resentment. Resentment places blame on others for either real or imagined injuries to us. But resentment only hurts us, as Eliphaz stated.

The comforting truth is that God is always in control. When He allows difficult people in our lives, He can speak to us even through them, if we learn to keep an open heart.

An open heart is one that is willing to learn, willing to confront its own sin, and willing to see more of God in every situation, especially the painful ones.

Isn't it ironic that Eliphaz was the one who said *resentment kills a fool?* If Job felt resentful toward anyone at that moment, it was probably Eliphaz. Yet when resentment takes hold in our lives, our hearts become closed to God. We can defeat resentment by acknowledging God's control over every detail. When God allows others to inflict pain on us, He will always give us more grace. He will strengthen us to forgive. As we keep an open heart toward God, we'll discover more about His unconditional love and forgiveness for us.

> **He will strengthen us to forgive**

As much as I didn't want to, I did finally follow the suggestion to get some counseling. Though it didn't change my physical condition, I learned some valuable things about God and about myself.

God wants us to have open, willing hearts. In Psalm 51:12b David prayed, *grant me a willing spirit, to sustain me.* When we have an open heart,

- God can use painful comments to lead us to deeper humility and compassion—making us more sensitive to the pain of others.
- He can turn resentment into forgiveness—giving us a deeper appreciation for His forgiveness toward us.
- He can turn our trials into opportunities—enabling us to show His grace to others. That's what God loves to do.

Thinking It Through:

a) How do you usually respond when someone makes an insensitive remark about the storm you're going through? Have you ever unintentionally made similar comments to someone else?

b) Are you struggling with resentment toward someone? Would you like to have an open heart instead? Talk to God about what you're thinking. Ask Him to give you a heart that is open and willing in every circumstance.

Seeing God Through The Storm

Chapter 9

Heal Me

In 2004 I faced health problems once again. This time my health completely collapsed, no hope of healing in sight. For two years I searched for answers, but I kept getting worse. On Thanksgiving Day I reached a point of desperation. I cried out to God, "I don't care what it takes or what I have to go through or what you have to do—just do something!" And He did.

However, God's answer to my prayer was not physical healing. Instead, He showed me how "sick" I was on the inside. I realized I'd been afraid of letting God expose my inner needs. I feared what He might show me about myself.

Thankfully, that day God gave me courage to let Him reveal what was inside my heart. And He gave me strength to ask Him to change me. That was the beginning of my inner healing.

If your storm is one of sickness, like mine, then you know what it's like to pray every day for healing. Yet, I think God is more focused on the health of our spirits. He often uses physical difficulties to show us how much we need His spiritual "doctoring." I've learned that what we all need, even more than physical healing, is healing in our spirits. Job was no exception.

Eliphaz had a mouthful of words that were no help to Job. Yet he did say something profound.

> *Blessed is the man whom God corrects; so do not despise the discipline of the Almighty.*
> *For He wounds, but He also binds up; He injures, but His hands also heal.*
> -Job 5:17-18

Many times God allows storms in our lives so He can bring the inner healing we need. When things are going well, it's easy to ignore or suppress any past hurts we haven't fully resolved. When a storm strikes, suddenly everything seems more difficult. The past can haunt us, the future frighten us. In that moment, God longs to display His healing power in our lives. If we've learned to keep an open heart toward Him, He can use our pain to bring healing.

Experiencing God's healing touch can look different from one person to another. But I think a few aspects of inward healing apply to us all.

1) Inner healing involves forgiveness.

Learning to forgive those who have wounded us and to receive God's forgiveness for our past sins are both vital for healing. This process is not easy. But it is possible by God's power and grace. As we give and receive forgiveness, God sets us free from bitterness, anger, regret, and guilt. Forgiveness is a powerful tool for healing.

2) Inner healing requires replacing my thoughts with God's thoughts.

Things people say to us or about us can unconsciously shape our view of ourselves, leading to insecurity or a distorted perception of who we are. God longs to replace these wrong thoughts with His thoughts about us. As He makes us aware of incorrect thoughts, we can intentionally focus on specific verses containing the truths we need—we are loved, accepted, forgiven, etc. Many times we must choose to believe what God says is true about us in spite of how we feel. Gradually the true and lovely thoughts from God's Word will bring the healing we need.

3) Inner healing includes focusing on the greater truth.

Some wounds in life are not caused by sin or wrong thoughts but from unavoidable loss, heartbreak, or tragedy. When we feel consumed with our painful situation, we can look for a greater truth to dwell on. I first learned this when I was eight and my father passed away. In the midst of my grief and tears, my mom comforted me. She reminded me that my dad was in heaven, and he was no longer sick but rejoicing with Jesus. As I focused on that greater truth of his life in heaven, it helped ease the pain of the lesser truth of his physical death. With God there is always a greater truth to comfort us. And in every situation, the promise of eternity with Jesus is a healing balm to our souls.

These three aspects of inward healing have helped me enormously. Yet there are some ways God brings healing that cannot be explained—because He is GOD. He works in supernatural ways. Psalm 147:3 says, *He heals the brokenhearted and binds up their wounds.* I've discovered that no matter what kind of inner pain, when I humble myself and ask God to heal it, He does.

I'm so thankful that when God heals a wound, it's truly healed—no more pain, regret, or guilt. God's healing power is even more effective than our bodies' ability to heal a cut. After the scab falls off a cut, the skin is as good as new, like it never happened. Or even if the cut scars, there's no longer any pain from it. When God heals something in our hearts, even if we remember the past, the pain is over.

Sometimes God heals our inner wounds immediately. Other times it's a gradual process of feeling less pain from day to day. Inner healing isn't something we can manufacture. It's a work God does in us. Only God can bring healing. Only He is our Healer.

Maybe you're wondering why God allows pain in our lives. Why doesn't He keep us from being wounded in the first place? I only know that all of us will be hurt at some point. That's life on earth. But we can choose how we'll respond to painful experiences. We can box them up and shove them to the back of our "mental closet," or we can admit they are there and bring them to God.

Isn't it amazing that God wants to heal our wounds? He could let us carry them around all our lives, like a backpack full of rocks. Instead He often orchestrates our difficult circumstances so we'll cry out for His healing touch.

God wants to heal our wounds

During the years of chronic illness, God brought many heart issues to my attention, things I had buried or ignored for years. He showed me the people I needed to forgive, the regrets I could let go, and the emotional pain He wanted to heal. As I spent time with Jesus and meditated on His Word, He set me free from past wounds.

At the same time, I learned that inner healing is an ongoing, life-long process. Even as I write this, God continues to reveal more areas in my heart that need healing. While we can experience God's healing and restoration day by day, I believe that perfect wholeness is reserved for eternity. When we get to heaven, all pain will be gone, all tears wiped away, every spirit totally healed!

Until then, these days and moments are our opportunity to get to know God as our Healer. If I had the choice of living the last several years over without the health trial but also without God's healing process in me, I know I would willingly go through the fire again. I'd choose it in order to experience God as my loving, faithful, gracious Healer.

I think Job would say the same about his experience.

When the pain of the past comes to the surface in your storm, remember God loves you. He cares about you enough to allow you to go through hardship in order to heal your heart and restore your soul.

I'm so glad He does! What is a storm compared to a spirit set free?

Heal us, Lord, we pray. Amen.

Thinking It Through:

a) Can you think of any emotional wounds from your past that you're still carrying around? Ask God to help you recognize the things in your heart that He wants to heal.

b) Pour out your heart to God right now about the wounds you know are there. Ask Him to encourage you from His Word and help you with practicing forgiveness, thinking His thoughts, and focusing on the greater truths. Pray for His healing touch to set you free from the pain of the past.

Seeing God Through The Storm

Chapter 10

No More

Sometimes the pain from our storm is so crushing that we can't hold on to God's perspective. We don't want to learn anything. We don't want to look for the good in our trial. We just want to say, "No more!"

Job felt like that.

> *If only my anguish could be weighed and all my misery be placed on the scales!*
> *It would surely outweigh the sand of the seas—no wonder my words have been*
> *impetuous. The arrows of the Almighty are in me, my spirit drinks in their poison;*
> *God's terrors are marshaled against me.*
>
> -Job 6:2-4

When we're being pounded by the storm, our words, like Job's, may be *impetuous*. I've experienced that. As my health deteriorated, I became too weak to speak or move off the couch. At the same time, our house was contaminated by toxins, and I couldn't stay there. I moved from place to place, staying with friends or sleeping in the car. Then I began having trouble breathing much of the time.

The stress of those days was overwhelming. Finally, I told God I didn't care anymore. I didn't care what His purpose was or what He could teach me. I didn't even care about my own life. I just wanted relief from the storm.

Though Job spoke impetuously out of his pain, he wanted something more than release from his agony. He expressed one desire.

> *Oh, that I might have my request, that God would grant what I hope for,*
> *that God would be willing to crush me, to let loose His hand and cut me*
> *off! Then I would still have this consolation—my joy in unrelenting pain—*
> *that I had not denied the words of the Holy One.*
>
> -Job 6:8-10

Job wanted to die. But his plea was motivated by more than longing for relief. Job recognized how weak he was, not only physically but also in his faith. He was afraid he couldn't endure much longer without losing his trust in God. Job believed it would be better to die while he still had his faith than to keep living and end up denying God.

Job's request may sound extreme, but he had great insight. Even the strongest faith can break down under intense suffering. Job had held on to this point, but he didn't think he could take any more. To Job, honoring God was more important than life.

In my stressful situation, I also wanted God to let me die, to just take me to heaven. For me and for Job, God's answer was the same—"No." Every time I told God, "I can't take it any longer. No more!" He replied, "Yes, you can. I will carry you through."

God knows exactly how much we can endure by His strength and grace. It's usually more than we think we can handle, but the LORD has promised to be all we need. When I look at Job and see how God sustained him through his incredible suffering, I find comfort. I know if God did that for Job, He can do it for me. And for you.

the LORD has promised to be all we need

After God brought me through those awful moments when I asked to die, I saw things more clearly. God knew it was my anguish speaking, not my heart. I'm glad He didn't let me die but instead sustained me through my suffering.

When you reach the point where all you can say is, "No more!" I pray you will hear God's loving reply: "I AM more—more powerful than your pain, more wise than your anguish, more gracious than your need."

Even to your old age and gray hairs I am He, I am He who will sustain you. I have made you and I will carry you; I will sustain you and I will rescue you.
-Isaiah 46:4

> **Thinking It Through:**

a) Have you been through a time when your storm was so bad you wanted to die? How did God bring you through it?

b) Do you feel like God is giving you more than you can bear right now? How does Job's story encourage you about God's ability to carry you through?

Enough

"That's enough. Just let me die,"
said Elijah, Jonah and Job.
How many times has it been said,
"I've had enough. No more!"
How many times has God replied,
"I AM enough, and more."

I've said it too, "Lord, that's enough!"
I've wept til I had no tears.
How many times has my heart cried,
"I can't take it anymore!"
And every time I hear Him say,
"I AM enough, and more."

Seeing God Through The Storm

Chapter 11

Forgiven

When it seems like there's no end to your storm, do you sometimes wonder if it's because God can't or won't forgive you for some sin? Have you ever prayed something like Job did?

> *If I have sinned, what have I done to you, O watcher of men? Why have you made me your target? Have I become a burden to you? Why do you not pardon my offenses and forgive my sins? For I will soon lie down in the dust; you will search for me, but I will be no more.*
> -Job 7:20-21

As Job's trial stretched on, he wondered if it was because God was withholding forgiveness for some reason. Job surely knew he was blameless before God (Job 1:1), yet in his anguish he questioned everything.

Job needed reassurance of God's forgiveness. He didn't have the life and words of Jesus to encourage him as we do. While Jesus was dying on the cross He prayed, *Father, forgive them* (Luke 23:34). Incredible! Jesus prayed for the very people who killed Him. How can we imagine that He won't forgive our sin?

Jesus died as the perfect sacrifice for all sin, so we could receive forgiveness. *In Him we have redemption through His blood, the forgiveness of sins, in accordance with the riches of God's grace* (Eph. 1:7).

No matter how we feel during times of suffering, we can know that God has forgiven us. The moment we trusted Jesus as our Savior, God forgave all our sin—past, present, and future. He forgave us, not because we deserved it, but because Jesus paid the price for our sin with His own life's blood. God no longer holds our sins against us.

No matter what sins are in our past, we will never have to face God's punishment for them. We are no longer condemned. *Therefore, there is now no condemnation for those who are in Christ Jesus* (Rom. 8:1).

When we question God's forgiveness, we are insulting Jesus and His incredible sacrifice for us. We are forgiven! Nothing can change that fact. God will not withhold His forgiveness from us—because Jesus earned it once for all.

After we're saved, we aren't instantly made perfect. We still sin. These ongoing sins cannot change our forever forgiven status with God. Yet, the choices we make day by day do affect our lives. God wants us to choose obedience and submission to Him, because He knows that's the best thing for us.

God is gracious and faithful to show us when we've sinned. Then the Holy Spirit enables us to repent—to change our thinking about ourselves and about our sin—so we won't continue in the same sins. When we recognize the lies attached to certain sins, then we can combat those sins with God's truth. God also works in us to change our desires, so we won't want to sin but will delight in doing what is right and good (Phil. 2:13).

When we recognize that we've sinned, we don't have to beg God to forgive us. Instead we can thank Him for forgiving our every sin at the cross (Col. 2:13-14). Knowing that the gift of forgiveness is forever ours in Christ empowers us to say "no" to sin and to live in peace and freedom.

If we choose to continue in willful disobedience to God, we will experience His discipline in some way. He disciplines us out of love, in order to draw us back to harmony with Him. God is even greater than the father in the story of the prodigal son (Luke 15:11-32).

> *So he got up and went to his father. But while he was still a long way off, his father saw him and was filled with compassion for him; he ran to his son, threw his arms around him and kissed him.*
> -Luke 15:20

Even before we turn to God, His heart is filled with forgiveness and love toward us.

Perhaps you know God has forgiven you, but you feel as though He doesn't like you. Too often we picture God's forgiveness the way other people forgive us. Sometimes people say "I forgive you, but…." Then they add something like:

- I don't want to talk to you right now.
- Don't bother me for a while.
- You need to make it up to me.

Human forgiveness is often conditional or limited. Not so with God.

1 Corinthians 13:4-8a says, *Love is patient, love is kind. It does not envy, it does not boast, it is not proud. It is not rude, it is not self-seeking, it is not easily angered, it keeps no record of wrongs. Love does not delight in evil but rejoices with the truth. It always protects, always trusts, always hopes, always perseveres. Love never fails.*

This passage doesn't only explain how to love others. It also describes the way God loves us. He doesn't keep a record of our sins, He doesn't hold our sins against us, He is patient and kind with us, and no sin can diminish His love for us. When God says, "I forgive you," there is no "but…."

When God says, "I forgive you," there is no "but…."

Sometimes even though we know God has forgiven us, we're still weighed down by guilt or regret. As God continued healing my heart, I realized I was carrying a burden of regret from a wrong choice that caused pain to someone I cared about. Though my friend forgave me and I knew God had forgiven me, I couldn't escape my regret. Eventually, God showed me that I was choosing not to accept His forgiveness. He reminded me, "That sin was paid for by the blood of my Son. It is washed away. Removed. Forgotten." I needed to believe that truth, receive it, and reject the feelings of guilt. When I did, I felt so free!

God's forgiveness is powerful. No matter how much or how often we sin, it is covered by God's unlimited forgiveness in Christ. And just as God forgives us freely, He will also empower us to practice forgiving others. He knows that forgiveness is something we all need.

God wasn't punishing Job or withholding His forgiveness, even though it felt that way to Job. Whenever you, like Job, have doubts about God's forgiveness, remind yourself, "That sin is washed away by the blood of Jesus." Trust God's Word and rejoice in the truth. You are eternally forgiven!

> *Praise the LORD, O my soul, and forget not all His benefits—*
> *who forgives all your sins and heals all your diseases...*
>
> *He does not treat us as our sins deserve or repay us according to our iniquities. For as high as the heavens are above the earth, so great is His love for those who fear Him; as far as the east is from the west, so far has He removed our transgressions from us.*
> -Psalm 103:2-3, 10-12

Thinking It Through:

a) Is there some sin from your past that you've thought God can't or won't forgive? What did you learn about God's forgiveness today that encourages you?

b) Take a few minutes to think about the verses used in this chapter. Share with God your thoughts about His gift of forgiveness. Ask Him to give you a forgiving heart toward others.

Seeing God Through The Storm

Chapter 12

God-Centered

"Why do bad things happen to good people?" You've probably heard this question as often as I have. The assumption behind it is that good things should happen to good people and bad things to bad people. That's only fair, right? Mankind has thought this way for thousands of years. Including Job's friends.

In his anguish, Job questioned everything. Instead of offering compassion and understanding to Job, his friends rebuked and insulted him.

> *Then Bildad the Shuhite replied: "How long will you say such things? Your words are a blustering wind. Does God pervert justice? Does the Almighty pervert what is right? When your children sinned against Him, He gave them over to the penalty of their sin. But if you will look to God and plead with the Almighty, if you are pure and upright, even now He will rouse himself on your behalf and restore you to your rightful place."*
>
> -Job 8:1-6

Bildad was convinced Job's children had sinned and that was why God destroyed them. He also assumed Job had sinned. Bildad's speech shows he had a wrong view of God. Bildad believed if Job repented, then God would restore him to the prosperity he had before—to his *rightful place*. To Bildad life was a basic formula—"if you sin, you'll suffer; if you're righteous, you'll prosper."

Bildad's philosophy is still common today. "If I'm a good person, then good things should happen to me." Do you know anyone who believes that? It sounds good. But is it accurate?

To answer this question we need to rethink the concepts of "good" and "bad." First, when we look at ourselves, no matter how good we think we are, none of us is actually good in God's eyes. To God, being good means being perfectly righteous. We all fall short of that. Isaiah 64:6 says, *All of us have become like one who is unclean, and all our righteous acts are like filthy rags; we all shrivel up like a leaf, and like the wind our sins sweep us away.* To a holy God, we are all bad people.

If we stand before God on our own, we have no rightful place. Our sins deserve only condemnation. Thankfully, when we received Jesus as our Savior, God not only forgave all our sins, He graciously clothed us in Christ's righteousness. That certainly isn't our rightful place. It isn't what we deserve—it's grace! In Jesus, we receive countless good things we could never earn, such as forgiveness, love, kindness, peace, joy, etc. Praise God that He gives bad people good things that only Christ deserves.

> **In Jesus, we receive countless good things we could never earn**

Second, when we look at our circumstances, we see that God can use even bad experiences for our good (Rom. 8:28). Joseph understood this truth. Though his brothers sold him into slavery, he said, *You intended to harm me, but God intended it for good…* (Gen. 50:20). What God allows in our lives isn't always easy or pleasant; sometimes it's painful. But He brings a good result from it (Heb. 12:11).

The problem with Bildad's view was that he looked at life from a man-centered perspective, not a God-centered one. If man is the center of our focus, then we define "good" and "bad" by what we think or feel. According to our standards, God should punish the bad people and reward the good people.

When God is at the center of our vision, we learn to let Him define what is good and bad. According to His standards we are all bad people, who by His grace are constantly receiving good things we don't deserve. And we know that the bad things we encounter, God will work for our good.

During my years of illness, it was hard for some of my friends to understand what God was doing in my life. They said things like, "You love God and want to serve Him. You don't deserve this trial." Though their intent was kind, they were thinking from a man-centered view. From God's perspective, I don't deserve a problem-free life because I love Jesus. Furthermore, I know that every problem the LORD allows in my life will ultimately be for my good. When I let Him define the terms, I move from a man-centered view to a God-centered one.

Job certainly had a more God-centered perspective than his friends. Bildad's only concern seemed to be Job's return to prosperity. He was stuck in his man-centered view of life. But God wasn't punishing Job. At the end of the book, we'll see that God allowed Job's bad trial in order to do something good in Job's life. For one thing, God used Job's circumstances to draw Job to a deeper intimacy with Him.

Whether we experience prosperity or pain, easy days or hard times, a God-centered perspective reminds us that God is always focused on our friendship with Him. With a God-centered view, we know that all things are a gift of God's grace—His kindness that we don't deserve.

Praise God that we don't live by a formula! We live in a relationship—with a gracious God. Knowing the LORD, receiving His grace, and enjoying Him in every circumstance is definitely not our *rightful place*. But aren't you grateful it's the place where we stand?

> *Therefore, since we have been justified through faith, we have peace with God through our Lord Jesus Christ, through whom we have gained access by faith into this grace in which we now stand. And we rejoice in the hope of the glory of God. Not only so, but we also rejoice in our sufferings....*
> -Romans 5:1-3

Thinking It Through:

a) Do you think your perspective recently has been man-centered or God-centered? Are you more concerned about your circumstances or your relationship with God?

b) Write a definition for grace in your own words. Think of a way God has used difficult times in the past to strengthen your relationship with Him. Thank Him that He desires a closer friendship with you.

Seeing God Through The Storm

Chapter 13

Surrounded

Through all the years I've struggled with serious health problems, I've never doubted God's power and ability to heal me. Yet at times I've wondered, "Lord, if you love me, why won't you heal me?" In a storm, we often recognize God's power, but we may find it hard to sense His love.

Job definitely had a more God-centered view than his friends, but he still had much to learn. In response to Bildad's speech, Job declared:

> *His [God's] wisdom is profound, His power is vast. Who has resisted Him and come out unscathed? He moves mountains without their knowing it and overturns them in His anger. He shakes the earth from its place and makes its pillars tremble. He speaks to the sun and it does not shine; He seals off the light of the stars. He alone stretches out the heavens and treads on the waves of the sea. He is the Maker of the Bear and Orion, the Pleiades and the constellations of the south.*
>
> -Job 9:4-9

Job could see God's power clearly. He knew that God is in control of everything, but it didn't comfort him. Without the assurance of God's love, the display of His power can be frightening. Job knew the LORD can do whatever He chooses, yet God had not chosen to restore him. In his despair, Job lost sight of God's love.

Have you ever been there? I have.

I'll never forget one horrible day. I was sick and miserable, and I was weary of being sick and miserable. I went to my mom in tears and asked, "What does God want from me? Why won't He heal me?" She just hugged me, cried with me, and reminded me once again that God still loved me, even though I couldn't sense it in that moment.

The fact is that God's love is as real as the air we breathe. We can't see the air or touch it, but we know it's real every time we take a breath. In a similar way, though we can't see God's love with our physical eyes or touch it with our fingers, we are surrounded by it always.

The Apostle Paul experienced all kinds of hardships and suffering. Yet he wrote these words:

> *Who shall separate us from the love of Christ? Shall trouble or*
> *hardship or persecution or famine or nakedness or danger or sword?...*
> *For I am convinced that neither death nor life, neither angels nor demons, neither the present*
> *nor the future, nor any powers, neither height nor depth, nor anything else in all creation, will*
> *be able to separate us from the love of God that is in Christ Jesus our Lord.*
> -Romans 8:35, 38-39

Nothing can separate us from God's love—not hardship, not persecution, not extreme suffering, not even death! Almighty God has wrapped us in His love through Jesus, and nothing will ever change that. It is an eternal reality. God loves you. God loves me. Always.

I think one reason we may not feel like God loves us is that we have such a limited concept of who God is. The more we get to know Him, the more we will grow in understanding His love. God's love is about more than making us feel good. It's about His transforming work in our lives. It's about showing us more of who He is. It's about lifting us above earthly attitudes to see eternal realities.

God's love is about more than making us feel good

Paul wrote that God's love *surpasses knowledge* (Eph. 3:19). Human intellect can never completely grasp the magnitude of the love of God. That's how profound it is! Yet God wants us to know and experience more of His incredible love for us. To our surprise, God often uses storms to reveal His love in a deeper way.

Seeing God Through The Storm

When life is going smoothly, we tend to think of God's love in shallow terms. We appreciate Him taking care of us or keeping problems away. But in the middle of a storm, we discover that we can take shelter in God's love. We can trust Him to meet our needs. We can rely on Him to give us strength one moment at a time. We can receive His divine comfort.

In trials, we experience different aspects of God's love as it becomes more real to us. And in those moments when we can't see or feel God's love, we learn to embrace it by faith.

In my misery and anguish, I had lost sight of God's love. I needed my mom to remind me that God hadn't stopped loving me. Looking back now, I can see many good things God brought out of my trial. I know the suffering He allowed was from His heart of love. I can also see many ways the Lord was expressing His love to me every day. Through my mom's selfless service in taking care of me, through e-mails from friends who were praying for me, through anonymous financial gifts, through songs I heard, and through books I read—God's love was always there surrounding me.

Job didn't have Paul's words in Romans 8 to remind him that not even his horrible agony could separate him from God's love. Yet when he looked back years later, I imagine Job saw the faithful love of God surrounding him through it all.

I'm so thankful that the love of God is a reality, no matter how we feel or what we're going through. Every trial is another opportunity for us to experience God's love in new and deeper ways than we have before.

When we see God's power displayed around us as Job did, I hope it will remind us of the power of His love as well—a love so strong that nothing can remove it, nothing can separate us from it, and nothing can keep it from surrounding us!

...the LORD's unfailing love surrounds the man who trusts in Him.
-Psalm 32:10b

> **Thinking It Through:**

a) Have you recently questioned God's love for you? What prompted you to do so?

b) When you think about God's love surrounding you, what is your response? Ask God to help you embrace the fact of His love by faith. Pray He'll open your eyes to see His expressions of love to you today.

Seeing God Through The Storm

Chapter 14

God's Heart

When we're languishing in a storm, it's tempting to base our beliefs about God on our circumstances or on our feelings. Yet many times those ideas are false. Perhaps this is another reason that God allows storms in our lives. In every situation, our heavenly Father wants us to surrender our opinions of Him and seek the truth about who He is—His heart.

In his trial, Job had lost sight of God's love. It seems that Job allowed his misery to blind him to truth.

> *Even if I summoned Him and He responded, I do not believe He would give me a hearing. He would crush me with a storm and multiply my wounds for no reason. He would not let me regain my breath but would overwhelm me with misery.*
>
> -Job 9:16-18

Job couldn't see God's love or mercy, so he assumed they were no longer there for him. I'm not discounting the reality of Job's suffering, but these words are only his opinion about God—based on his feelings at the moment, not based on the truth.

When our opinions about God are wrong, as they often are, they pull us away from Him. Consider Job's words from chapter 23: *He carries out His decree against me, and many such plans He still has in store. That is why I am terrified before Him; when I think of all this, I fear Him* (Job 23:14-15).

Job didn't actually know what God's plans for him were, but when he assumed they were harmful, he became afraid of God. Instead of looking for the truth about who God is, Job let his opinion keep him bound by fear. God doesn't want us to be afraid of Him. He does want us to "fear" Him—to have a correct understanding of who He is.

Seeing God Through The Storm

Proverbs 9:10 tells us that *The fear of the LORD is the beginning of wisdom, and knowledge of the Holy One is understanding.*

So how do we gain a correct understanding of God? How do we find the truth about who He is? We find it by reading the book He wrote. God isn't hiding from us. He has gone to great lengths to give us the Bible with all its wonderful revelation about His character and His ways. Every chapter, every verse, tells us something about who our God is. The Bible is our eternal source of truth.

We also find the truth about God by looking at Jesus. Hebrews 1:1-3a says, *In the past God spoke to our forefathers through the prophets at many times and in various ways, but in these last days He has spoken to us by His Son…The Son is the radiance of God's glory and the exact representation of His being….* Jesus came to reveal God. The fact that Jesus humbled Himself to become a man and live on earth shows us clearly that God longs for us to know Him.

God longs for us to know Him

To look past our circumstances and understand God's heart, we need to keep our attention on Jesus. We need to continually read what God has written about Himself in the Bible. God is not inconsistent like us—kind one moment and selfish the next. God is always the same loving, faithful, sovereign, good, gracious God He has declared Himself to be. Sometimes we feel like that's true, sometimes we don't. But neither circumstances nor feelings can change what is true about God.

In the past eight years of illness, there were several times that my family and friends held a special day of prayer for my healing. And three times we asked the elders of our church to pray over me. Almost every time, I actually felt worse soon after. Judging by my circumstances, it might seem like God was being unkind—we prayed earnestly for healing, and I got worse.

In those moments, I could have assumed God was taunting me. At times I was tempted to think that way. Thankfully, I was getting to know God better during those years. I was learning to trust His heart.

Job made assumptions about God's character based on his circumstances. Yet, God doesn't treat us that way. 1 Samuel 16:7 says, *The LORD does not look at the things man looks at. Man looks at the outward appearance, but the LORD looks at the heart.*

God does not judge us by our outward appearance. Neither should we form ideas about God based on our circumstances or how we feel in the moment. Let's not allow pain to rob us of truth. Let's seek to know the LORD better, discover His heart, and trust Him for who He is.

Thinking It Through:

a) List some of your current opinions about God. Do you think they're all accurate? Are they based on the truth in the Bible or on how you feel?

b) List some things about God that you know are true from what He says in the Bible. Talk with the Lord, telling Him that however your circumstances may appear right now, you want to trust His heart.

Seeing God Through The Storm

Chapter 15

Unlimited

Are you feeling pressed and squeezed by your storm today? Is it all around you, suffocating you, never-ending?

I've had days like that. Thankfully, my mom always reminds me that the storm won't last forever. It does have a limit.

I imagine that Job felt like his trial would never end. As if Job didn't have enough agony, his third friend, Zophar, added more negative comments.

> *Then Zophar the Naamathite replied: "Are all these words to go unanswered?*
> *Is this talker to be vindicated? Will your idle talk reduce men to silence?*
> *Will no one rebuke you when you mock?"*
> -Job 11:1-3

You'd think Job's friends could have shown some compassion. Instead they continued to fire their opinions at him. However, even in their criticism, God was at work. Consider this significant part of Zophar's speech.

> *Can you fathom the mysteries of God? Can you probe the limits of the Almighty?*
> *They are higher than the heavens—what can you do? They are deeper than the depths of the grave—what can you know? Their measure is longer than the earth and wider than the sea.*
> -Job 11:7-9

Isn't that beautiful? In essence, Zophar was saying that God has no limits. God is infinite!

While our storms can sometimes feel like they are endless, they really aren't.

Everything in our world has its limits. The ocean is only so deep. The temperature can only get so hot or so cold. The lifespan of every creature is only so long. Only one being truly has no limits—God Almighty.

No human mind can fully comprehend infinity. When the writers of the Bible tried to express this concept, they could only compare God to created things that are very large or long or wide, like the ocean or the skies.

Try, just for a moment, to wrap your brain around this idea: God has no limits.

Is your head hurting yet?

Even though we can't fully understand this truth, it can be a great comfort to us. For instance, God's love has no limits. That means He will never run out of love. He will never stop loving you! His love for you will always be as great as it has always been.

God's power has no limits. Nothing or no one is as powerful as God. When He displays His power it isn't used up like ours is. He doesn't have to take a break and recharge His batteries. And nothing is too hard for Him. Parting the Red Sea was just as easy as making a donkey talk or giving you strength to do the dishes. Nothing is too hard for the LORD, and nothing is too small to bother Him with. He has no limitations.

> ***Nothing is too hard for the LORD...***
> ***He has no limitations***

When I was a teenager living in Colombia, I often slept outside under the stars. We lived miles from the city, tucked in a little valley with nothing to obstruct our view of the heavens. I loved to gaze up at the night sky. There were more stars than I've ever seen anywhere else, a seemingly limitless number of them shining down on me. Underneath that glorious canopy, I felt an overwhelming sense of awe. And that is just a taste of how we should feel when considering God's unlimited nature.

The more I think about God's infinity, the more amazed and grateful I am! As we go through storms, we can apply this truth to whatever we're experiencing.

- Are you discouraged? God's encouragement is ongoing and eternal—He will encourage you (2 Thess. 2:16-17).
- Are you in need? God's ability to provide has no restrictions—He will meet all your needs (Phil. 4:19).
- Are you feeling weak? God's strength has no end—He will sustain you (Is. 40:28-31).

In every hardship, God's grace has no boundary—it is always sufficient for us. Our circumstances, our storms, our trials are limited. But God is not!

I wonder if Zophar had any idea what he was really saying in those few verses. Even if he didn't, God knew that one day we would read Zophar's words and find comfort in their truth.

I'm so glad that God is not like us, limited as we are. Even though I can't fully grasp His infinity, what I can understand of it gives me courage and hope. Our God has no limits. Hallelujah!

Thinking It Through:

a) What are you worrying about today? Does your worry indicate an area of God's character that you're thinking of as limited? How can seeing that same attribute as unlimited encourage you in your storm?

b) Spend some time worshipping God for His unlimited attributes that mean the most to you right now.

Seeing God Through The Storm

Chapter 16

God's Wisdom

In 2008 I was finally diagnosed with Environmental Illness (E.I.). One of the challenges of living with E.I. is keeping a "safe" environment at home (no chemicals, perfumes, mold, etc.). For months I'd slept in the largest bedroom in our house because it was the safest one for me. Then some toxic fumes contaminated our garage, which shared a wall with my bedroom. It was so bad that I had to move into the back bedroom on the other side of the house.

This may not sound like a big deal, but it was very difficult for me. Being exposed to the toxic fumes left me extremely weak and barely able to breathe, with a headache the size of Australia. Still, I helped my mom move everything—all the books, clothes, and furniture—out of the back bedroom. We washed the walls, put my mattress on the floor, added an air purifier, and I settled into my new home.

I was not happy with God. I vented my anger and misery at Him. "What are you thinking, Lord? Why are you doing this to me?"

However, after a couple of weeks, my body recovered from the toxic fumes, and I noticed something. My new bedroom was a much safer place for me. It had fewer smells since I was farther from the garage, less electrical fields, more sunlight, etc. I'd been angry with God, but ultimately what He allowed was exactly what I needed. Of course we don't always see things this clearly in every trial. But remembering this experience helps me when I start to feel angry or question God.

Because God is infinite and we are finite, we often don't understand what He's doing. When we question why He allows difficult circumstances or why He acts differently than we expect Him to, we are questioning His wisdom. In the midst of our doubts, fears, anger, and questions, we desperately need to be reminded of the perfect wisdom of God.

I think of God's wisdom as the fact that God knows what He is doing. His knowledge is unlimited—He knows all there is to know about everything. He knows what is best for me in every situation. You and I only know some things. We can only see so far. God sees everything from the beginning of time throughout eternity.

God is the source of all wisdom. Even in his pain, Job recognized this.

Where then does wisdom come from? Where does understanding dwell? It is hidden from the eyes of every living thing, concealed even from the birds of the air... God understands the way to it and He alone knows where it dwells, for He views the ends of the earth and sees everything under the heavens. When He established the force of the wind and measured out the waters, when He made a decree for the rain and a path for the thunderstorm, then He looked at wisdom and appraised it; He confirmed it and tested it. And He said to man, "The fear of the Lord—that is wisdom, and to shun evil is understanding."

-Job 28:20-28

Job understood that all wisdom comes from God. And for us, wisdom is acknowledging God for who He is. Wisdom is learning to "fear" the Lord—not to be afraid of Him, but to remember that He is God and we are not. Whatever happens in our lives is not by chance. God isn't scrambling around trying to figure out what to do next. He knows exactly what He's doing and why. We may not understand it, but that's okay. We can learn to trust God's wisdom and rest in Him.

In my search for answers to my health problems, I consulted more than 40 doctors in eight states. Most of them were no help; some even made me worse. I experienced a lot of pain, frustration, stress, and financial loss from their lack of wisdom. What I needed was a doctor who knew more than I did, a doctor with true wisdom.

The problem for many of us is that spiritually we try to be our own doctors. As a result we often make things worse. No matter how much we think we know, we don't know everything. Thankfully, we don't need to know everything! We do need to trust the perfect wisdom of our heavenly Father.

Even when life doesn't make sense, even when circumstances are painful or difficult, God can be trusted to do what is best for us. His knowledge and wisdom are perfect. Knowing this, we can view our storms as opportunities for seeking God and letting Him teach us what we need to learn. Many of the storms I've experienced were worth the pain because of what God taught me through them. Would I have chosen them? No. But I'm thankful God knew better than me what I needed. And I'm glad He always knows exactly what He's doing.

> **God can be trusted to do what is best for us**

There's so much about God, about life, and about ourselves that we don't understand. Sometimes God gives us the answers we seek. Other times He asks us to simply trust His divine wisdom. It's not clear if Job ever saw the whole picture of what was happening in his story, but he said, *To God belong wisdom and power; counsel and understanding are His* (Job 12:13).

When I'm tempted to question God or tell Him my "better" plan, I try to remember how He has proved His wisdom to me in the past. He knows what He's doing. I may not have all the answers, but I pray for strength to keep trusting my infinite God who is perfect in wisdom.

> *Oh, the depth of the riches of the wisdom and knowledge of God! How unsearchable His judgments, and His paths beyond tracing out! "Who has known the mind of the Lord? Or who has been His counselor?" "Who has ever given to God, that God should repay him?" For from Him and through Him and to Him are all things. To Him be the glory forever! Amen.*
> -Romans 11:33-36

Thinking It Through:

a) Have you been relying on your own limited wisdom or acting as your own spiritual doctor? Write your definition of God's wisdom. Why is it better to trust God's wisdom than to rely on your own understanding?

b) Looking back, think about a time when you saw God's wisdom in allowing a specific trial in your life. Ask your heavenly Father to overcome any anger or fear you may be experiencing in your storm right now. Pray for Him to strengthen your trust in His wisdom today.

Seeing God Through The Storm

Chapter 17

Intimacy

Some days even though I believe God knows what He's doing, I feel like He's too hard on me. I can't imagine how Job must have felt, since his suffering was so much worse than mine.

Job knew many wonderful truths about God, but he was in such agony that he kept returning to the idea that God was out to get him.

> *Why do you hide your face and consider me your enemy? Will you torment a windblown leaf? Will you chase after dry chaff?*
> -Job 13:24-25

I suppose Job had every reason to feel like God hated him. Yet even in his darkness, Job believed God wouldn't completely reject him.

> *If only you would hide me in the grave and conceal me till your anger has passed! If only you would set me a time and then remember me! If a man dies, will he live again? All the days of my hard service I will wait for my renewal to come. You will call and I will answer you; you will long for the creature your hands have made.*
> -Job 14:13-15

Job believed God's anger at him would eventually pass, and then God would long for Job again. I wish I could have been there to tell Job one of the most precious truths I've ever learned—God always longs for us!

God never tires of us or pushes us away from Him. He continually yearns for us to be close to Him, as He said in Jeremiah 31:20, *Therefore my heart yearns for him; I have great compassion for him.*

More than yearning for us, God actually pursues us. We are the ones who hide, fear, neglect, reject, or rebel against God. He is the one who initiates, draws, calls, reaches out, and pursues us with His love.

Think back through the stories in the Bible.
- Adam and Eve hid—God called out to them.
- Jonah ran—God brought him back.
- Peter denied Jesus—Jesus forgave and restored him.

Story after story illustrates God's loving pursuit of sinful people.

God created us to have intimate friendship with Him. He provided the Bible, sent Jesus to die for our sins, gave us the Holy Spirit to live in us, and much more. God pursues a close relationship with us not because we're irresistible (we're clearly not), but because He delights in lavishing us with His love and grace.

God does not need us. But He does long for us.

God does not need us. But He does long for us.

I can't put into words the amazement I feel that the LORD Almighty longs for me—that He wants to be my friend, that He enjoys me, that He yearns for me more than I could ever long for Him!

Is it hard for you to see God this way? Perhaps you've always thought of Him as distant or unapproachable. But it's true—God does long for you. He wants you to be close to Him, no matter how you may feel right now.

Consider what Jesus said about the people in Jerusalem, the ones who later killed Him.

> *O Jerusalem, Jerusalem, you who kill the prophets and stone those sent to you,*
> *how often I have longed to gather your children together, as a hen gathers her chicks*
> *under her wings, but you were not willing!*
> -Luke 13:34

Jesus knew the people were going to reject Him, still He longed for them to come to Him. God never stops longing for us even when we reject Him, run from Him, rebel against Him, or try to hide from Him. And when we respond to God's loving pursuit, we'll discover that He can use everything in our lives to develop a greater intimacy with us.

One of the things God uses is suffering. We may feel like our storm indicates that God is against us, but suffering is actually God's invitation for us to come closer to Him.

Jesus lived a life of hardship and suffering. How can we expect to know Him intimately without experiencing suffering like He did? The Apostle Paul wrote, *I want to know Christ and the power of His resurrection and the fellowship of sharing in His sufferings…* (Phil. 3:10). In our suffering we can understand more of who Jesus is and what He has done for us. Suffering can lead us to an intimacy with Jesus that we'll never know in a problem-free life. This isn't an easy process, but the reward is worth the pain.

- When I felt misunderstood or rejected by people who couldn't understand my illness, Jesus reminded me that even His own family didn't believe in Him.

- When I spent months moving from place to place, unable to live at home, Jesus reminded me that for three years He had no place to lay His head (Matt. 8:20).

- When my body was in pain and there was nothing I could do about it, Jesus reminded me that He willingly subjected His body to the pain of the cross—for me.

These are only a few examples of how Jesus has taught me to share in the fellowship of His sufferings. By pointing me to His own pain and hardships, Jesus took my focus off myself and helped me receive His comfort. In everything we suffer, we have the opportunity to encounter Jesus and come to know Him better than before.

Job was wrong about God being angry with him. I don't think Job understood God's desire for intimacy with His people. Elihu also missed this important truth. He said, *Out of the north He comes in golden splendor; God comes in awesome majesty. The Almighty is beyond our reach and exalted in power* (Job 37:22-23a).

Yes, Almighty God is awesome and exalted. But He is not beyond our reach. He has chosen to make Himself accessible to us. Our God desires intimacy with us. He wants us to come to Him, to know Him, and to enjoy fellowship with Him—especially in the storm.

God longs for you. How will you respond?

> *Here I am! I stand at the door and knock. If anyone hears my voice and opens the door, I will come in and eat with him, and he with me.*
> -Revelation 3:20

Thinking It Through:

a) Have you ever considered the fact that God longs for you? Think back over your life and describe some ways that God has pursued you with His love.

b) Ask yourself: How would my life be different if I believed that God longs for me? Write a prayer to the Lord expressing your thoughts. Ask Jesus to help you experience a deeper, more intimate friendship with Him in every situation.

Seeing God Through The Storm

Chapter 18

For Me

Do you know someone who is praying for you today? In the intensity of the storm, when it feels like so much is going against us, it's a great comfort to know someone is on our side, someone is **for us.**

I've been blessed to have hundreds of people praying for me during my ongoing health trial. Many times when I was weary and discouraged, I received e-mails from friends reminding me they were praying for me. Knowing I had such support encouraged me to keep enduring.

Maybe you've experienced that same comfort from the prayers and support of others. Yet even if you feel like no one is praying for you, that you're completely alone, there's always one person that is on your side—God Himself.

As far as we know, Job didn't have a single person praying for him or supporting him. His children were gone. His "friends" were against him with their repeated accusations. His wife was no help. Job didn't think he could talk with God either.

> *He [God] is not a man like me that I might answer Him, that we might confront each other in court. If only there were someone to arbitrate between us, to lay his hand upon us both, someone to remove God's rod from me, so that His terror would frighten me no more. Then I would speak up without fear of Him, but as it now stands with me, I cannot.*
>
> -Job 9:32-35

Job felt like God was against him, but he couldn't take God to court as though He were a man. No, God is Almighty. Job could never earn an audience with this supreme ruler. He needed someone to be his mediator, his advocate, his go-between.

This need haunts all of us before we are saved. We're all sinners, unable to represent ourselves before a perfect and holy God. Job seemed to understand that only God could provide a mediator. In Job 17:3 he said, *Give me, O God, the pledge you demand. Who else will put up security for me?*

What a miracle that out of His great love God Himself became our mediator! Jesus left heaven, came to earth, lived a sinless life, and willingly died as the perfect sacrifice for all sin. As our mediator, He is the one who brings us to God. Clothed in Christ's righteousness, we are joyfully accepted and unconditionally loved by Almighty God. We no longer need to fear anything because we are on God's side—and He is on ours. The LORD is **for us**!

> *What, then, shall we say in response to this? If God is for us, who can be against us? He who did not spare His own Son, but gave Him up for us all—how will He not also, along with Him, graciously give us all things? Who will bring any charge against those whom God has chosen? It is God who justifies. Who is he that condemns? Christ Jesus, who died—more than that, who was raised to life— is at the right hand of God and is also interceding for us.*
> -Romans 8:31-34

Jesus is not only our mediator, He is also our intercessor. Hebrews 7:24-25 says, *but because Jesus lives forever, He has a permanent priesthood. Therefore He is able to save completely those who come to God through Him, because He always lives to intercede for them.* Jesus knows every detail of our lives. He sees our hearts. And He prays for us.

Jesus is praying for us

I can't grasp all that this means; in some ways it's a mystery. But I'm always encouraged by this wonderful truth. Jesus became our mediator so that we can have intimacy with a holy God. And Jesus is our constant intercessor. When we feel alone, or if we don't know how to pray, we can trust that Jesus is praying for us. The Holy Spirit also intercedes for us (Rom. 8:26-27).

The whole trinity—Father, Son and Holy Spirit—is now involved in our lives. God loves us, has saved us, prays for us, answers prayer for us, and graciously gives us all things. God has made it abundantly clear that He is **for us**!

Job's emotions told him that God was against Him. Yet at the same time, Job realized that only God was purely righteous and able to be his advocate, his mediator, and his intercessor. Job's complaint was toward God, but his hope was also in God. He said, *Even now my witness is in heaven; my advocate is on high. My intercessor is my friend as my eyes pour out tears to God; on behalf of a man He pleads with God as a man pleads for his friend* (Job 16:19-21).

No matter what we're going through or how we feel, the truth is that God is never against us. He is always for us! And He will continue to be for us every day of our lives. That's who He is.

Thinking It Through:

a) Have you ever imagined what it would be like to try to approach God without Jesus, totally on your own? What does it mean to you that Jesus is your mediator, that in Him you can approach God as a welcome and beloved friend?

b) Do you have a hard time believing that God is for you? Read Romans 8:31-34 again. Choose the part that encourages you the most and write it on a piece of paper or note card. Place it where you'll see it often to remind yourself that God is for you.

Seeing God Through The Storm

Chapter 19

True Justice

While I know my ongoing health trial is part of God's plan for me right now, sometimes I still envy others. It's hard to watch many healthy people waste their lives on pointless pursuits. I often wonder, "Why do I have to suffer while they take their health for granted?" Maybe you've had similar thoughts about your own situation. It's tempting to question God's justice when we compare our situation to those around us.

Job had to face his own questions about God's justice as well as his friends' accusations. He pleaded with his friends for compassion instead of condemnation.

> *Then Job replied: "I have heard many things like these; miserable comforters are you all! Will your long-winded speeches never end? What ails you that you keep on arguing? I also could speak like you, if you were in my place; I could make fine speeches against you and shake my head at you. But my mouth would encourage you…."*
>
> -Job 16:1-5

Job was right when he called his friends *miserable comforters*. They continued to argue with him using the same evidence to make their point. First Eliphaz spoke again. *All his days the wicked man suffers torment, the ruthless through all the years stored up for him* (Job 15:20). Next Bildad chimed in (Job 18:2, 5). Then Zophar added his comments (Job 20:28-29). Basically they kept pounding on the same nail: the wicked will experience all kinds of terrible circumstances and perish. Since Job experienced terrible circumstances, they concluded he must be wicked—because God is not unjust.

I wonder if these men were as convinced as they sounded. Had they never observed how many wicked people were prospering? Had they really never seen a godly man have troubles? Perhaps they only saw what they wanted to see.

Job noticed the prosperity of the wicked. He asked his friends, *Why do the wicked live on, growing old and increasing in power? They see their children established around them, their offspring before their eyes. Their homes are safe and free from fear; the rod of God is not upon them* (Job 21:7-9).

If God allows the wicked to prosper and the godly to suffer, it brings us to the question, "Is God really just?" In spite of how I may feel at times, I know the answer is, "Yes, God is just."

I think there are two main problems for us when we think about God's justice.

First, we want to see justice right now. However, since God is eternal, His justice is ultimately worked out in eternity. Sometimes we see justice carried out on earth, but many times we have to wait for eternity when God will judge all men.

Though my health collapsed in 2004, I didn't immediately face the fact that I was seriously ill and my recovery would take years. Finally, I accepted reality and applied for disability benefits. My mom and I filled out a mountain of paperwork, sent it in and waited. Months later we received a reply: application denied. We appealed it and waited. Again: denied. Even though I was clearly too sick to work, and we had evidence to prove it, the system would not grant me the disability benefits I deserved.

So we hired a lawyer, who filled out more paperwork, which was again denied. For the final appeal I had to appear before a judge who would decide my case once for all. My lawyer came armed with a file folder of evidence four inches thick. I was so weak I could hardly sit up, but I did my best to answer the judge's questions. I made it through the hearing, and two weeks later we got word that the judge approved my claim! After two and a half years, I finally had justice. The system had denied me, but the judge did what was right.

Right now you and I live in the messed-up system of this sinful world. Many people who deserve punishment live prosperous lives. Others who do good suffer or are persecuted. But one day we'll stand before the Righteous Judge who will deal justly with all men. Hallelujah!

The second problem we have with God's justice is reconciling it with His grace. Every day God offers grace, through Jesus, to a sinful world. If God executed perfect justice now, who would be saved? Are we not all sinners in need of God's grace? The truth is that none of us would want to experience God's justice without first having received His grace.

While we are often frustrated by unfairness in life or grieved by painful injustice around us, we can be grateful that God graciously reserves complete justice for eternity.

Though Job questioned God's justice, I think he understood that in eternity God makes everything right. Job said, *God drags away the mighty by His power; though they become established, they have no assurance of life* (Job 24:22). The wicked may prosper for a while, but they have *no assurance of life.* The righteous may suffer on earth, but as Paul wrote, *I consider that our present sufferings are not worth comparing with the glory that will be revealed in us* (Rom. 8:18).

God is just. And He is gracious. During the years I waited for disability, God provided for my needs in miraculous ways. Although I had debt from medical bills, when I received the back payments of disability, the amount covered my debt with some left over! In a similar way, God's grace is sufficient to sustain us in an unjust world as we wait for the perfect execution of His justice in eternity. One day we'll stand before the righteous Judge and receive the rewards of heaven. We'll experience God's presence and His finger tenderly wiping away every tear from our eyes. In that moment, every injustice of this lifetime will fade away.

in eternity God makes everything right

> *And I heard a loud voice from the throne saying, "Now the dwelling of God is with men, and He will live with them. They will be His people, and God Himself will be with them and be their God. He will wipe every tear from their eyes. There will be no more death or mourning or crying or pain, for the old order of things has passed away."*
> -Revelation 21:3-4

> **Thinking It Through:**

a) How does seeing God's justice as eternal help you find peace about the way things are now?

b) In what area of your life have you been questioning God's justice? Share your heart with Him in prayer. Then be still and listen to what He will say to you.

Seeing God Through The Storm

Chapter 20

Brokenness

The knowledge of God's eternal justice can comfort us in our storm. Whatever trials we're going through now, we have an eternity of perfect happiness to look forward to. There are times though, when that doesn't seem like enough. What are we supposed to do in the meantime? Is there nothing good in store for us while we're still on earth?

Job asked similar questions. He said, *My days have passed, my plans are shattered, and so are the desires of my heart* (Job 17:11). Whatever good waited for him in eternity, Job felt he had nothing left on earth. His plans were shattered; his desires were dead. Job was a broken man.

Do you feel like Job? Does your life seem broken, shattered, empty?

As months of illness turned into years, I watched my world slowly collapse. My plans dissolved. My dreams for ministry, family, friendships, even little things like learning guitar, one by one went up in the smoke of my deteriorating health. My dreams died, and with them a part of me died too. I felt I had nothing left, just an empty heart crying out to God.

I know this breaking process isn't something any of us would choose. Being broken involves dying—to one thing or many things. Ultimately it means accepting death of self. Paul wrote, *I have been crucified with Christ and I no longer live, but Christ lives in me. The life I live in the body, I live by faith in the Son of God, who loved me and gave Himself for me* (Gal. 2:20).

When we trusted Christ as our Savior, our sinful nature was spiritually crucified, meaning it's no longer a dictator over us. However, it isn't eradicated. We're still attached to it. Many times our sinful nature influences us so that we choose self over Jesus.

In His faithfulness, God allows hardships in our lives to bring us to the point of brokenness. True brokenness is total abandonment of ourselves. It is unconditional surrender to Christ. In accepting brokenness, we willingly accept the death of self—death to our own will. Only when self has been dethroned in our hearts, can we learn how to let Jesus live His life through us.

Through the agony of my illness, God was, in a sense, crushing me. But He wasn't destroying me. He used a painful breaking process to show me my own heart—my selfish motives, self-righteousness, and self-reliance. When I was healthy and active, I rarely paid attention to those things. In my weakness, I couldn't ignore them. When I reached the place where I had nothing left of myself to rely on, I finally realized that Jesus is all I need.

I've heard it said that every person who is greatly used by God is first deeply broken by God. I believe it! I wanted to serve God with my abilities and passions. I wanted to do things my way, in my own strength. God wanted me to abandon my own will and seek His will.

- He wanted me to learn how weak I am, so He could fill me with His strength.
- He wanted me to stop looking to things or people to fill my heart and let Him alone satisfy me completely.
- He wanted me to die to myself so that Jesus could reign in me!

Coming to the point of brokenness is painful, but it is necessary. Jesus said, *I tell you the truth, unless a kernel of wheat falls to the ground and dies, it remains only a single seed. But if it dies, it produces many seeds* (John 12:24). Brokenness is not a punishment—it's a preparation.

After death comes new life. When we accept death of self, God teaches us how to walk in His life. God must bring each of us to the place where He is all we have and all we desire. Then we'll be ready for Him to use us in ways we never imagined.

brokenness is the path to fruitfulness

Living in dependence on Jesus instead of relying on self is a lifelong journey. One that begins with brokenness. As God pours His life into our hearts, we'll see Him do more through us than we could ever do on our own. That's why brokenness is the path to fruitfulness.

God took Job through a more difficult breaking process than anyone else has probably ever experienced. Job literally had nothing left, only anguish. But the LORD wasn't finished with Job. Job didn't know the rest of his story. He had no idea of the fruitful future God had in store for him. I don't think we do either.

God has good plans for us while we're on this earth—but they are His plans, not ours. Through brokenness we learn to lay down our desires, our lives, our self. Then we can offer our broken pieces to God. As He reshapes them by His grace, we'll be amazed at the magnificence of the plans and Christ-filled life God has in store for us.

To be powerfully used by God requires brokenness. But take heart! Brokenness is the beginning of something beautiful.

Thinking It Through:

a) Do you think God is using your storm as a breaking process in your life? Are you resisting brokenness or are you willing to accept it even though it's painful?

b) Write a list of your dreams and desires that you feel God has shattered. By faith, offer up your list to God. Ask Him to fill your broken, empty heart with Himself. Then trust the LORD to work out His good plans for you in His perfect timing.

Broken To Beautiful

Broken, shattered,
Pieces scattered.
Is this my life?
Dreams have crumbled,
Idols tumbled.
Nothing left.

Nail-scarred hands,
Heart that understands,
You hold my life.
Healer of the broken,
Truth you've spoken,
You're all I need.

My pieces repairing,
While broken, preparing
A new life for me.
The best plan you weave,
Help me receive,
Your will for me.

Transformed through the pain,
No longer the same,
You are my life.
Your grace shining through,
You change broken to
Beautiful.

Seeing God Through The Storm

Chapter 21

Hope

Living with chronic illness is a constant battle against discouragement and despair. For years I kept hoping I'd find some answers, hoping my health would improve, hoping my circumstances would change. Instead, day after day, doctor after doctor, treatment after treatment, I seemed to grow worse. Finally I gave up in resignation. "This is my life. Why bother hoping anymore?"

Have you experienced a similar hopelessness in your storm? In the midst of Job's breaking process, he experienced despair and hopelessness.

If the only home I hope for is the grave, if I spread out my bed in darkness...
where then is my hope? Who can see any hope for me?
-Job 17:13, 15

Job had no hope. He was simply waiting for his miserable life to end. Without hope that's where we are, too. Hope is what motivates us to keep going; it enables us to get out of bed in the morning. Without hope we are just waiting to die.

When the Bible talks about hope, it doesn't mean wishing for something to happen. It means having a confident expectation in what we know is true. If we only have "hope" (wishful thinking) in circumstances or people, we will continually be disappointed. But we can always have genuine hope (confidence) in our God.

We can hope in God in the darkness because of what we know is true about Him:
- God is in control.
- He is always good.
- His love surrounds us.
- He has a plan and purpose for us.
- He is working out His plan and purpose both now and for eternity.

There are many precious truths about God that we can hold onto in the storm. Which ones immediately come to your mind?

Paul wrote about hope in suffering.

> *And we rejoice in the hope of the glory of God. Not only so, but we also rejoice in our sufferings, because we know that suffering produces perseverance; perseverance, character; and character, hope. And hope does not disappoint us, because God has poured out His love into our hearts by the Holy Spirit, whom He has given us.*
> -Romans 5:2b-5

As Christians we have been given the hope—confident expectation—of one day sharing God's glory in heaven. We can always rejoice in that hope! However, we can also rejoice in our sufferings. Why? Because suffering is a tool God uses to work a beautiful transformation in our lives.

When we submit to the Lord in our sufferings, He teaches us perseverance. As we rely on God's strength to persevere, He builds the character of Christ in us. And when the character of Christ fills our lives, we live in continual hope.

This process teaches us that nothing else, no one else, is truly dependable. Circumstances come and go, people can fail us, our own strength gives out. But God never changes. In suffering we can discover the rock-solid character of God. And when our hope is in God, we'll never be disappointed.

> *when our hope is in God, we'll never be disappointed*

This foundation of hope in God rather than earthly things can also give us hope for our storm. Hope comes from remembering what is true.

- God is all-powerful, with Him all things are possible (Matt. 19:26). We have **hope** that God can change any situation.
- God is faithful. When the LORD chooses not to change our situation, we know He is developing perseverance in us (Jam.1:2-4). We have **hope** that the Lord can use our circumstances to change us.

- God is gracious. As He changes us, others will be affected (Phil. 1:12-14). We have **hope** that even in the midst of our storm, God will bless others through us.

Whatever trials we experience, we can have hope in our unchanging God. The storm won't last forever. For some, it may continue until the moment they step into eternity and see Jesus face to face. For others, the end of the storm is not so far away… though a new storm may soon appear on the horizon. Because storms come and go and come again, placing our hope in God is vital. Only He never changes.

In my days of despair, God graciously helped me place my hope solely in Him. Eventually, He also gave me hope for my circumstances. Though I was still sick and miserable, I finally had hope that someday I could get well.

I've learned that no matter what we're experiencing, we can have hope—confident expectation—based on who God is and what He has promised.

God is our hope even when it seems nothing is left for us but death. In spite of feeling hopeless, Job knew that God was the only one he could hope in. Job believed his trial would only end at his death. Still he declared: *Though He slay me, yet will I hope in Him* (Job 13:15a).

As the storm rages around you, you may feel like you have nothing left, no hope. But with the LORD, you don't have to succumb to hopelessness. In those dark moments of despair, when all hope seems gone, let the light of God's truth shine on you. You may not know what will happen next, but you do know who your God is. He is your hope.

For you have been my hope, O Sovereign LORD, my confidence since my youth…
But as for me, I will always have hope; I will praise you more and more.
-Psalm 71:5, 14

> **Thinking It Through:**

a) Lately, what has been the basis of your hope—wishing your circumstances would improve or confidence in who your God is? Which kind of hope will help you most in your storm right now?

b) List some truths about God that you can focus on today to strengthen your hope in Him. Can you say, *Though He slay me, yet will I hope in Him,* as Job did? Remember, when we are faithless, the LORD is still faithful (2 Tim. 2:13).

Seeing God Through The Storm

Chapter 22

Faith

It amazes me that, despite everything he went through, Job never lost his faith in God. Yes, he questioned God, he despaired over his circumstances, and he complained about injustice. But he never denied God or turned away from Him. Instead Job proclaimed:

> *I know that my Redeemer lives, and that in the end He will stand upon the earth. And after my skin has been destroyed, yet in my flesh I will see God; I myself will see Him with my own eyes—I, and not another. How my heart yearns within me!*
>
> -Job 19:25-27

Job didn't say, "I think my Redeemer lives…" or "Maybe I'll see Him…." No, he said, *I **know** my Redeemer lives…I myself will **see** Him.* That's faith!

Hebrews 11:1 tells us that *faith is being sure of what we hope for and certain of what we do not see.* Faith isn't pretending, wishful thinking, or make-believe. Faith is being certain about what is true. Faith is agreeing with an invisible reality. Job didn't have all the answers, but he was sure and certain about his Redeemer who keeps His word.

Though we can see the evidence of God's power and work around us, we cannot literally see Him. Because God is infinite and we are finite, because He is Spirit and we are flesh, because He is the Creator and we are His creation—the only way we can relate to Almighty God is through faith.

Thankfully, faith isn't something we have to conjure up on our own. It's a gift God gives us (Eph. 2:8). God Himself enables us to have faith. When we received God's gift of salvation, it was by faith. In that moment, we were certain the gospel is true. We didn't think, "It's probably true," or, "It's a good bet." No. We were so certain that we staked our eternal destiny on the truth of the gospel. That's faith.

Salvation is only the starting point of our faith journey. For the rest of our earthly lives, we experience God's process of expanding our faith. He wants us to become certain about more and more truths, such as His constant presence, His perfect wisdom, and His unconditional love. And God often uses trials to build our faith.

During easy times, we may see evidence of God's presence, love, or power in our lives. But when a storm comes, we can feel like all our "faith-supports" are gone. We don't see God anywhere. This is the place where faith can grow. The Apostle Peter understood this.

> *...though now for a little while you may have had to suffer grief in all kinds of trials. These have come so that your faith—of greater worth than gold, which perishes even though refined by fire—may be proved genuine and may result in praise, glory and honor when Jesus Christ is revealed.*
> -1 Peter 1:6-7

Trials prove and grow our faith. I was taught many good truths about God when I was young, and I believed them. As I got older, various storms assailed me. I wrestled with the knowledge of truth in my head until it became a choice of my will. I chose to believe the truth, regardless of what I could or couldn't see. And one by one the truths I was taught moved from being knowledge in my head to being sure and certain in my soul.

God often uses trials to build our faith

Trials are God's tool. Through them He teaches us to trust the truth of who He is and what His Word says. Our faith expands as we become more aware of what is unseen. Faith does not come naturally. It must be encouraged and exercised by the grace of God. Through studying God's Word, getting to know Him better, and learning to trust

Him in trials, I've watched God gradually expand my faith. The Lord also strengthens our faith as we recognize His faithfulness to us, both past and present.

Why does God take us through this painful faith-building process? Peter said that it's because our faith is more valuable to God than gold is valuable to men! Our faith in God will bring Him praise, glory, and honor. Trusting the LORD, though we cannot see Him, is the ultimate compliment. Seeing what is unseen by faith honors God and demonstrates to other people that our God is worthy of trust.

Many things in life can draw our attention, but the most important thing to focus on is what we can't see with our physical eyes. Learning to see God in our storm means being more aware of what is invisible than what is visible. It means being certain of what we know is true. Everything we see or feel with our senses will one day pass away. What we can't see, God and His truth, is the ultimate reality that will last for eternity.

Job couldn't see God anywhere in his trial, but he declared by faith that one day he would see the LORD. Job's faith was being tested and proved, but there's no doubt that he came forth as gold.

> *So we fix our eyes not on what is seen, but on what is unseen.*
> *For what is seen is temporary, but what is unseen is eternal.*
> -2 Corinthians 4:18

Thinking It Through:

a) What does it mean to you to "live by faith"? How has God used various trials in your life to expand your faith in Him?

b) How can you learn to be more aware of what is unseen? Thank Jesus that He is the author and perfecter of your faith (Heb. 12:2). Ask Him to help you fix your eyes on what is invisible—who He is—one day at a time.

Seeing God Through The Storm

Chapter 23

Glory And Honor

In the ongoing search for answers to my health problems, my mom found a clinic in Dallas that specializes in Environmental Illness. We drove from Florida to Dallas, but as soon as I walked into the clinic I had trouble breathing. I was severely allergic to something in the building and couldn't stay there for treatment. Another patient told us of a similar clinic across town. But that doctor's treatments made me even worse. We tried a third doctor, who bluntly asked me, "Do you really want to get well?" Then she decided she couldn't help me.

We were frustrated and discouraged! All our time, effort, and money seemed wasted in this fruitless search for help.

As I prayed about the third doctor's question, I realized something. As much as I did want to get well, restored health was not my main goal. The Lord had changed my heart. Now my primary goal was to honor God—whether healthy or sick. I learned this from Paul's example.

> *I eagerly expect and hope that I will in no way be ashamed, but will have sufficient courage so that now as always Christ will be exalted in my body, whether by life or by death. For to me, to live is Christ and to die is gain.*
> -Philippians 1:20-21

It would have been easy for me to stay discouraged and self-absorbed in my illness. But I knew God wanted me to refocus on honoring Him.

In spite of everything Job suffered, he held on to his faith. But he lost his God-centered focus.

> *As surely as God lives, who has denied me justice, the Almighty, who has made me taste bitterness of soul, as long as I have life within me, the breath of God in my nostrils, my*

lips will not speak wickedness, and my tongue will utter no deceit. I will never admit you are in the right; till I die, I will not deny my integrity. I will maintain my righteousness and never let go of it; my conscience will not reproach me as long as I live.
-Job 27:2-6

Job knew he had not acted wickedly or done anything to deserve his affliction. However, his defense sounds like it was all about Job. ***I*** *will not deny* ***my*** *integrity…* ***I*** *will maintain* ***my*** *righteousness.* Instead of praying that God would be honored, Job became focused on himself.

Job's three friends were no help. They continued to harass him.

Then Eliphaz the Temanite replied: "Can a man be of benefit to God? Can even a wise man benefit Him? What pleasure would it give the Almighty if you were righteous? What would He gain if your ways were blameless?"
-Job 22:1-3

A little later Elihu added his thoughts.

If you sin, how does that affect Him? If your sins are many, what does that do to Him? If you are righteous, what do you give to Him, or what does He receive from your hand? Your wickedness affects only a man like yourself, and your righteousness only the sons of men.
-Job 35:6-8

It sounds like these men tried to convince Job that God didn't care whether he lived a righteous life or a wicked one. Since God is Almighty, why should anything we do matter to Him?

Oh, how wrong they were!

We know that God created us for His glory (Is. 43:7), and He takes pleasure in us (Zeph. 3:17). The way we live matters to God. However, with our human mindset, we often try to honor God by measuring our behavior with some standard of godliness we determine. If we do enough good things or if we have good intentions, we think we're honoring God.

Paul's words in Romans 7:18 give us a different perspective. *I know that nothing good lives in me, that is, in my sinful nature. For I have the desire to do what is good, but I cannot carry it out.* Our efforts to honor God in our own strength are futile because there is nothing good in our sinful nature. Jesus said, *I am the vine; you are the branches. If a man remains in me and I in him, he will bear much fruit; apart from me you can do nothing* (John 15:5).

We honor God, simply and only, by letting Jesus live His life through us.

I think God often allows hardships in our lives so we will recognize our own weakness and stop trying to honor God with our self-effort. Paul wrote about his experience with this.

> *We honor God...by letting Jesus live His life through us*

> *...there was given me a thorn in my flesh, a messenger of Satan, to torment me. Three times I pleaded with the Lord to take it away from me. But He said to me, "My grace is sufficient for you, for my power is made perfect in weakness." Therefore I will boast all the more gladly about my weaknesses, so that Christ's power may rest on me. That is why, for Christ's sake, I delight in weaknesses, in insults, in hardships, in persecutions, in difficulties. For when I am weak, then I am strong.*
> -2 Corinthians 12:7b-10

Paul recognized that he was only strong in Christ's power. Therefore he boasted in his weaknesses because in them Jesus would be honored.

My natural inclination is to try to honor God with my strengths and abilities. But God's way is to use trials, hardships, and weaknesses to teach me to abandon my own efforts and let Christ's power live through me.

God is honored, not by my weak attempts to measure up to some standard, but by my heart's response to Him. Even when I'm too weak to move off the couch, I can still honor God—

- by saying, "Not my will, but yours be done,"
- by asking Jesus to give me His thoughts and desires,

- by resting in Jesus' life and power at work within me.

God is worthy of honor and glory every moment because of who He is. The wonder is that He has chosen to display His greatness in and through you and me. We didn't seek Him—He sought us. We didn't love Him—He first loved us. We cannot glorify Him in our own strength—He is the one who empowers us to submit to Him, to trust Him, and to honor Him.

It is still a mystery to me that Almighty God who is continually worshiped and adored by angels, would choose a messed-up sinner like me to display His power and bring Him glory. Not only that, but as others have seen my weakness and Christ's power at work in my life, they have been drawn to God as well.

I don't fully understand this gift, but I want to embrace it. I don't want to stay self-absorbed like Job was in his pain. I want to say, "Lord, here I am. Teach me to let Christ live through me. Take my weakness and my suffering and use it for your glory."

When, by Christ's power, we trust God in the darkness, praise Him in the storm, or offer up the tiniest speck of faith in the wilderness—He is honored. Even when no one else sees, in the smallest act of turning our hearts toward Him, God is glorified. By His grace at work in us, He will receive glory and honor through our lives, even in the storm.

> *For from Him and through Him and to Him are all things.*
> *To Him be the glory forever! Amen.*
> -Romans 11:36

Thinking It Through:

a) Have you ever thought, "What I do or believe doesn't really matter to God"? What do you think now?

b) Have you been trying to honor God in your own strength? Spend some time in prayer. Ask God to teach you how to let Christ live through you. Thank Him for the privilege of glorifying Him in any situation through your heart's response to Him.

Seeing God Through The Storm

Chapter 24

Most Valuable

Do you ever think back to how life was before your storm? Do you miss the way things used to be? I miss little things like driving a car, doing jigsaw puzzles, and playing the piano. I miss important things like going to church, celebrating holidays with my family, and having energy to play with my nieces and nephews. I'm thankful I have many good memories from before I got sick to look back on. Sometimes remembering the good times helps distract me from my current misery. Other times it just leaves me discontent with the present.

In Job's final speech, he spoke about how much he longed for the "good old days."

How I long for the months gone by, for the days when God watched over me, when His lamp shone upon my head and by His light I walked through darkness! Oh, for the days when I was in my prime, when God's intimate friendship blessed my house, when the Almighty was still with me and my children were around me, when my path was drenched with cream and the rock poured out for me streams of olive oil.
-Job 29:2-6

Notice some other things Job said he missed.

When I went to the gate of the city and took my seat in the public square, the young men saw me and stepped aside and the old men rose to their feet... Whoever heard me spoke well of me, and those who saw me commended me... Men listened to me expectantly, waiting in silence for my counsel. After I had spoken, they spoke no more; my words fell gently on their ears. They waited for me as for showers and drank in my words as the spring rain. When I smiled at them, they scarcely believed it; the light of my face was precious to them. I chose the way for them and sat as their chief; I dwelt as a king among his troops; I was like one who comforts mourners.
-Job 29:7-8, 11, 21-25

It's hard for us to fully grasp how drastically Job's life had changed. In our culture it might be like the President suddenly becoming chronically ill, alone, and homeless. Job had been honored and looked to as a ruler. He was a righteous man who used his influence for good. However, once his circumstances changed and he experienced affliction, people turned from respecting him to mocking him. *But now they mock me, men younger than I, whose fathers I would have disdained to put with my sheep dogs* (Job 30:1). It's no surprise Job lamented his situation and wished his life could be like it was before.

I wonder though, what did Job miss the most? His wealth and comfortable life? The respect and admiration of those around him? Being with his children? Or did he miss most of all *God's intimate friendship* (Job 29:4)?

Clearly Job felt like God was no longer friendly toward him. *I cry out to you, O God, but you do not answer; I stand up, but you merely look at me. You turn on me ruthlessly; with the might of your hand you attack me* (Job 30:20-21). Was missing God's friendship even worse to Job than his deep loneliness or his extreme physical pain? *I have become a brother of jackals, a companion of owls. My skin grows black and peels; my body burns with fever. My harp is tuned to mourning, and my flute to the sound of wailing* (Job 30:29-31).

We don't know what Job missed the most or what was most valuable to him. But as I think about Job, I wonder about myself. What is most valuable to me? Is it comfortable circumstances? Approval from others? Being with loved ones? Or intimacy with God?

Have I let God's gifts become more important to me than God Himself?

Imagine a husband whose wife goes to visit relatives for a week. When she returns he exclaims, "Oh, Honey, I missed the clean clothes you always have for me, I missed how you keep me organized, and I especially missed your great cooking." How do you think the wife would respond? She'd be insulted, even heartbroken! She'd probably reply, "So you missed all the things I do for you, but you didn't miss me?"

I've learned that God wants me to love and adore Him for Himself, not for what He can do for me. This isn't because He's selfish. The LORD knows that the highest and greatest joy we'll ever experience comes not from enjoying His gifts but from enjoying Him!

Psalm 37:4 says, *Delight yourself in the LORD and He will give you the desires of your heart.* Jesus said the greatest commandment is to *Love the Lord your God with all your heart and with all your soul and with all your mind and with all your strength* (Mark 12:30).

Consider this: God is the source of all there is—He created everything. Doesn't it make sense then that while created things can bring us some joy, only the marvelous Creator will bring us the greatest joy? God wants us to value our relationship with Him above all else, because He knows that is what is absolutely the best for us.

> **only the marvelous Creator will bring us the greatest joy**

When the Lord removes some of the good gifts we're used to—whether it's possessions, health, prestige, or even people we love—I hope we'll hear Him calling to us in the midst of our pain. "My child, I am what you need. Let me be the most important One in your life."

Perhaps later on Job did decide his friendship with God was what he missed the most. God allowed Job's terrible storm, at least in part, to develop a deeper intimacy with Job. God wanted Job to recognize the LORD—not His blessings—as most valuable.

I still miss the many good things I've had to live without in this trial. But I've gained so much more in intimacy with the Lord. I've learned to say with Paul, *I consider everything a loss compared to the surpassing greatness of knowing Christ Jesus my Lord...* (Phil. 3:8).

Whatever our storm, whatever good things we miss, I pray we'll always be able to say, "Lord, You are most valuable to me."

Thinking It Through:

a) What have you been missing most in your current storm? Have you at times viewed those things as more valuable than your relationship with God?

b) Do you believe that knowing and enjoying God is the greatest happiness you can experience? Why or why not? Ask God to teach you how to truly delight yourself in Him whatever your circumstances.

Seeing God Through The Storm

Chapter 25

Motivation

How often do you stop to think about why you do what you do? Many of us live on autopilot much of the time. We move from task to task with hardly a moment to stop and think. We react to people and situations without realizing why. We repeat the same actions out of habit, unaware of what drives us, of our inner motives. I lived like this for many years, until the Lord began to show me that why we do what we do—our motivation—is important to Him.

After Job finished his lament, he made his final statement of innocence. He listed in detail the good things he had done and the wicked things he had not done. He also explained the motivation for his blameless lifestyle. *For I dreaded destruction from God, and for fear of His splendor I could not do such things* (Job 31:23).

Job knew God is holy and He will punish the wicked. So Job was determined to live a righteous life. However, I think Job's motivation was missing something. He had lived a righteous life out of respect for God and fear of the destruction that comes to the wicked. Yet in spite of his blameless ways, he experienced affliction—the loss of his family, wealth, and status. No wonder Job's wife told him to curse God and die. She probably thought, "What's the point of living righteously if you still end up with nothing?" What Job feared happened to him in spite of his righteous life. So why bother to keep obeying God?

That's a good question. What is our motivation for following God? Do we obey Him out of fear? Do we follow Him for what we'll get out of it? Motivation matters. When a storm strikes, our motive for following Jesus will either carry us through or leave us adrift. If we only follow God out of fear or from a desire for blessings, then when we experience pain or lose those blessings, it will shake our faith. We'll have no reason to go on.

One day when I was very ill and struggling to take each breath, I asked myself, "Why am I still following Jesus? Why don't I just give it up?" Aside from the obvious reason that I need God desperately, I was surprised by the answer my heart whispered back to me. "Because I love Him."

> *"I'm following the LORD because I love Him!"*

I love Jesus so much that I cannot imagine my life without Him! Even if it means more years of suffering, I want to go where He goes, to follow where He leads, to stay close to His heart.

I haven't always felt this way. It was a process. As God took me through one trial after another, He taught me more about Himself in each storm. The better I knew Him, the stronger my love for Him became, until the day my heart declared, "I'm following the LORD because I love Him!"

Perhaps this is the motivation Job was missing. We can't really blame him. He didn't have the Bible or the words of Jesus to reassure him in his storm. Yet I believe that God's desire was to change Job's motivation from fear to love.

It seems strange that God would use affliction—the very thing Job feared—to accomplish this change of heart. It reminds me that God's ways are not our ways (Is. 55:8). Job needed to see more of God before he was ready to move from fear to love. When we let God reveal Himself to us in the storm, He can bring the needed transformation to our hearts.

The Apostle Paul endured one storm after another, yet he kept following Jesus. I love the final sentence of his letter to the Ephesian Christians. *Grace to all who love our Lord Jesus Christ with an undying love* (Eph. 6:24).

Only God can give us an undying love for Him. And when love is the motive of our hearts, we'll find His grace sufficient to keep us following Him through every storm.

Thinking It Through:

a) Until now what do you think your motivation for following God has been? Today, if someone asked you, "Why are you still following Jesus?" what would be your honest answer?

b) Think back over the last few weeks. As you've seen more of God in your storm, do you think your love for Him has grown? Thank God for what He is doing in your life. Ask Him to keep transforming your heart and increasing your love for Him.

Seeing God Through The Storm

Chapter 26

God Speaks

Sometimes in the midst of the storm, it seems like God is silent. We call out to Him, yell at Him, or beg Him to act, yet there's no reply. If you've experienced something like this, you can imagine how Job felt.

Perhaps God's apparent silence was even more difficult for Job than his physical agony. For several chapters Job cried out to God, grieving over his situation, pleading for answers. Job's friends condemned him. God remained silent. So Job made his final defense for his innocence, then he had nothing more to say. God hadn't answered his questions or brought him relief. What else could he do?

Job had complained, questioned, begged, and wept until he was empty. His three friends finally stopped arguing with him. Then someone else spoke up.

> *So these three men stopped answering Job, because he was righteous in his own eyes. But Elihu...became very angry with Job for justifying himself rather than God. He was also angry with the three friends, because they had found no way to refute Job, and yet had condemned him. Now Elihu had waited before speaking to Job because they were older than he. But when he saw that the three men had nothing more to say, his anger was aroused.*
>
> -Job 32:1-5

Elihu was no kinder to Job than the other three men had been. He said, *Oh, that Job might be tested to the utmost for answering like a wicked man! To his sin he adds rebellion; scornfully he claps his hands among us and multiplies his words against God* (Job 34:36-37).

However, in the midst of Elihu's tirade, we once again find a gem of truth.

> *Why do you complain to Him that He answers none of man's words? For God does speak—now one way, now another—though man may not perceive it.*
>
> -Job 33:13-14

God does speak.

We may not always be perceiving, but God is always speaking.

God speaks to us through His creation (Rom. 1:19-20). Take a minute to consider the tree outside the window, the clouds drifting overhead, or the flower blooming among the weeds. God's creation daily demonstrates who He is—His character and His ways (Ps. 19:1-3).

God is also speaking through the Bible (2 Tim. 3:16). We have pages and pages of God's Word that He has spoken to His people over thousands of years. No matter what we're going through, there is something in God's Word that will speak to our need.

John 1:1 says, *In the beginning was the Word, and the Word was with God, and the Word was God.* As the Living Word, Jesus is continually speaking.

We may feel like God is silent, ignoring us, or has forgotten us, but that is not true. God could never forget us (Is. 49:15). His love never ignores us. And it is God's very nature to speak. Our role is to keep learning how to listen.

For many people, listening is a lost art. It's easier to talk. Listening to God requires even greater effort than listening to people because we can't audibly hear God's voice. Being still and listening with our spirits goes against our natural tendencies to keep busy or to surround ourselves with

it is God's very nature to speak

noise. Most often God speaks in a quiet voice, which we won't hear unless we cultivate a listening heart.

In my illness I've had a lot of time to practice listening to God. As I lay on the couch day after day, too weak to speak, God was the only one I could talk to. I directed almost all my thoughts toward Him. Little by little, He has taught me how to listen to His side of the conversation.

In the last few years, I've spent a lot of time reading the Bible. Being familiar with God's Word helps me discern when God is speaking to my heart or when I'm hearing some other voice. God will never speak anything to us that contradicts what the

Bible teaches. God's voice is the voice of truth. Jesus said the Holy Spirit would speak to us and make the truth known to us (John 16:12-15). We learn to hear God's voice by knowing His Word and by relying on the power of the Holy Spirit.

Another thing that helps me listen to God is the habit of asking Him questions—and then expecting to hear from Him.

- I begin each day by asking God what He wants me to do that day, then waiting on Him to guide my thoughts.
- When people say upsetting things to me, I pray, "Lord, is what they're saying true? What do you want me to learn from this?"
- If I have a decision to make, I ask God what His will is and wait for His guidance.

We can know we've heard God's voice when His peace reigns in our hearts. As long as there is confusion, frustration, or conflict within us, we probably haven't heard clearly from God. Yet He doesn't always speak in the way we expect or give us the answers we want. At times I've asked God to explain a situation in my life, and instead He convicted me of a sin in my heart. He knew I needed a pure heart more than an explanation. But He did speak to me.

Listening to God doesn't fit a formula. Primarily God speaks to us through the Bible. But as we learn to recognize His voice, He can also speak to us in unexpected ways. Sometimes God has spoken to me through a song, a painting, a person's comments, even a dream. With the Holy Spirit living inside us, we always have the ability to hear God's voice. However, there will always be competing voices, so it's important to ask God to make us better listeners.

Perhaps at times we don't want to listen to God because we're afraid of what He'll say. I feel that way sometimes. But even when I don't like what God speaks to me, I've discovered it's always worthwhile to listen to Him. About three and a half years into my health trial, God spoke to me through this verse: *Do not be afraid of what you are about to suffer* (Rev. 2:10a). I clearly heard the Lord speak those words to me personally. At first I was encouraged—I didn't need to be afraid! Then the second part of His message sunk in—my trial wasn't over yet. I still had more suffering to endure. That was not something I wanted to hear, but God knew I needed to hear it. I needed to prepare my mind for more suffering. God knew what anguish I would experience in the following months and years. He graciously gave me this warning, along with the encouragement not to be afraid.

I believe God is always speaking in one way or another. Learning to perceive His voice is an ongoing process. Thankfully, He is a patient teacher. When He seems silent, don't despair. Ask the Holy Spirit to help you listen, to open your ears to the ways God is speaking to you—perhaps through the love of other people, through a gentle breeze, or through a child's laughter. Keep reading God's Word, keep asking Him questions, and keep expecting to hear His voice. *For God does speak—now one way, now another…* (Job 33:14).

As we learn to listen and hear the LORD speaking, we will be transformed. We will grow in intimacy with the Almighty. We will find what we need in our suffering.

I am the good shepherd…
My sheep listen to my voice; I know them, and they follow me.
-John 10:14a, 27

Thinking It Through:

a) Do you think it's true that God is always speaking? Why or why not? Do you want to hear from God or are you afraid of what He might say?

b) Describe some ways God has spoken to you in the past—through His Word, the Holy Spirit, a friend, creation, or other ways. Ask your Good Shepherd to keep teaching you how to listen to His voice.

Seeing God Through The Storm

Chapter 27

Look Around

Do you sometimes feel enveloped by the cloud of your own suffering, until you can't see anything else? I think Job did. He needed a different view. Sometimes we do, too.

Elihu was right that God does speak. When all the men had finished their speeches, God finally spoke to Job. *Then the LORD answered Job out of the storm...* (Job 38:1).

Yet when God spoke, He didn't say anything we might have expected. God didn't commend Job's faith. He didn't give Job an explanation. He didn't offer sympathy. Instead, the LORD asked Job a series of questions that pointed Job to creation.

Who shut up the sea behind doors when it burst forth from the womb...
when I fixed limits for it and set its doors and bars in place, when I said,
"This far you may come and no farther; here is where your proud waves halt"?
Have you ever given orders to the morning, or shown the dawn its place...
Have you entered the storehouses of the snow or seen the storehouses of the hail,
which I reserve for times of trouble, for days of war and battle?
-Job 38:8-12, 22-23

God set limits for the ocean; He gives orders to the sun; He controls the weather. God has the power to do whatever He desires. When we see the evidence of His power in creation, can we not trust that He is in control of the circumstances in our lives?

God continued.

Can you bring forth the constellations in their seasons or lead out the Bear with its cubs?
Do you know the laws of the heavens? Can you set up God's dominion over the earth?...
Who endowed the heart with wisdom or gave understanding to the mind? Who has the
wisdom to count the clouds? Who can tip over the water jars of the heavens...?
-Job 38:32-33, 36-37

In wisdom God has established the universe and keeps it running. As we observe God's wisdom in creation, can we not trust Him to order our lives by the same wisdom?

The LORD asked Job more questions.

> *Do you hunt the prey for the lioness and satisfy the hunger of the lions when they crouch in their dens or lie in wait in a thicket? Who provides food for the raven when its young cry out to God and wander about for lack of food?*
> -Job 38:39-41

God provides food for His creatures whether powerful lions or tiny birds. In light of His faithfulness to the animals, can we not trust that the Lord will provide for us as well?

God still wasn't finished.

> *She [the ostrich] treats her young harshly, as if they were not hers; she cares not that her labor was in vain, for God did not endow her with wisdom or give her a share of good sense. Yet when she spreads her feathers to run, she laughs at horse and rider. Do you give the horse his strength or clothe his neck with a flowing mane? Do you make him leap like a locust, striking terror with his proud snorting?*
> -Job 39:16-20

The LORD has different purposes for His different creatures, and He gives them different abilities. Knowing this, can we not trust that God has given us what we need to fulfill His purpose for our lives?

When we see God's awesomeness displayed in creation, are we wise enough to acknowledge that we too are His creatures—subordinate to Him, dependent on Him, created to glorify Him?

Through creation we get a glimpse of God's power, His wisdom, His faithfulness, His provision for His creatures, and so much more. As Job heard God's questions, I imagine he felt quite small. God reminded Job of who He is—the LORD God Almighty! God basically told Job to look around him. Consider creation and see the LORD.

Seeing the reality of who God is in His creation reminds us of who He is in our lives as well. We all need to take time,

Consider creation and see the LORD

especially during a storm, to look around us and be in awe at the greatness of our God.

During the months I traveled from place to place consulting various doctors, the Lord gave me a special blessing—a visit to the Grand Canyon. It would be hard for anyone to stand on the edge of that chasm and not be in complete awe. Words can't describe it. Pictures can't do it justice. It's truly breathtaking.

There are a few buildings and shops on the rim of the canyon. At the entrance to one of them I noticed a plaque with this inscription:

> O LORD,
> *How manifold are thy works!*
> *In wisdom hast thou made them all:*
> *the earth is full of thy riches.*
> Psalm 104:24

> Father Almighty, wonderful Lord,
> Wondrous Creator, be ever adored;
> Wonders of nature
> Sing praises to You,
> Wonder of wonders –
> I may praise too!

Let us never forget who our God is—the Almighty Creator, worthy of praise!

I think God answered Job's questions with His own questions because He knew they would lead Job to the ultimate answer—"I AM." Like Job, this may not be the answer we were looking for, but in the end, it's the only answer we truly need.

Thinking It Through:

a) What attributes of God do you see in these passages from Job 38 and 39? How do you think you would have responded to God's questioning if you'd been in Job's place?

b) Is the cloud of self-focus still surrounding you today? Take some time to step outside and look around. Ask God to open your eyes to see Him in His creation and to remember that He is GOD.

Seeing God Through The Storm

Chapter 28

Tremble

God often uses storms to get our attention. When we take time to look around, we're reminded of who the LORD is. This knowledge leads us to deeper humility. Though, as Job discovered, it's not always a pleasant experience.

Job wasn't prepared for how God spoke and what He said. Every time I read this passage, I think this is the moment God will say "It's okay, Job. All this trouble wasn't your fault. Let me explain what's been going on…." Instead God said, *Who is this that darkens my counsel with words without knowledge? Brace yourself like a man; I will question you, and you shall answer me* (Job 38:2-3).

Even if God didn't give Job a full explanation, at least He could have offered Job some words of comfort and reassurance. But He didn't. God's approach at this point in the story always seemed harsh to me. Instead of consoling Job, God interrogated him.

> *Where were you when I laid the earth's foundation? Tell me, if you understand. Who marked off its dimensions? Surely you know! Who stretched a measuring line across it?*
>
> -Job 38:4-5

"Can you do this…? Do you know that…? Where were you when…?" In the final chapters of Job, it feels like God was pummeling Job with questions.

> *The LORD said to Job: "Will the one who contends with the Almighty correct Him? Let him who accuses God answer Him!" Then Job answered the LORD: "I am unworthy—how can I reply to you? I put my hand over my mouth. I spoke once, but I have no answer—twice, but I will say no more."*
>
> -Job 40:1-5

Job knew when to be silent, and this was definitely one of those times. But God wasn't finished yet.

> *Then the LORD spoke to Job out of the storm: "Brace yourself like a man; I will question you, and you shall answer me. Would you discredit my justice? Would you condemn me to justify yourself? Do you have an arm like God's, and can your voice thunder like His? Then adorn yourself with glory and splendor, and clothe yourself in honor and majesty. Unleash the fury of your wrath, look at every proud man and bring him low...crush the wicked where they stand...Then I myself will admit to you that your own right hand can save you."*
>
> -Job 40:6-14

How would you have felt in that moment?

I wouldn't have wanted to be in Job's place that day. Job had complained that God wasn't answering his cries. But when God did speak to him, it wasn't at all what Job expected. What could he do? How could he reply?

Faced with the majesty and grandeur of God, there is only one response—to tremble.

Notice that God spoke to Job *out of the storm*. Why did God choose a storm to speak to Job? Why not a gentle whisper like Elijah heard (1 Kings 19:9-13)? Or a burning bush like Moses experienced (Ex. 3:1-15)?

No. God used a storm—something we associate with power, even fear. Was God angry with Job? Was He trying to scare Job? We can't answer those questions, but we can remember that God loved Job. And Love always knows what we need. Sometimes we need a gentle whisper, at other times a powerful rebuke. God knew Job's heart. He knew what Job needed most. Job needed to be reminded of the awesomeness of Almighty God. He needed to stop complaining, arguing, and justifying himself and simply tremble before the LORD.

Have you ever had one of those fall-on-your-face moments when you were overwhelmed by the powerful reality of who God is? At times an intense awareness of God's holiness and my own sinfulness has left me trembling before Him. I've felt my unworthiness in God's presence so deeply I couldn't lift my head.

I didn't exactly enjoy those moments. I don't like being humbled. But many times God knows that's what I need. He's not being harsh. He knows what is best for me. He humbles me because He loves me. God says, *This is the one I esteem: he who is humble and contrite in spirit, and trembles at my word* (Is. 66:2b). The LORD honors those who tremble before Him.

Love always knows what we need

Maybe you've felt like Job. Or perhaps you've read this passage and thought God was unfair to Job. The truth is that God loved Job enough to speak to him in the way and with the words Job needed.

When you hear the LORD speaking with a voice of thunder instead of a gentle whisper, remember that God loves you. And Love knows what you need. Don't run away from the humbling experience. Fall on your face and tremble before the LORD. He will lift you up again.

Humble yourselves before the Lord, and He will lift you up.
-James 4:10

Thinking It Through:

a) Are you surprised by how God spoke to Job and what He said? Have you ever felt like God treated you in a similar way?

b) Whether God speaks to you in a gentle whisper or through a storm, can you trust that it's because He loves you and knows what's best for you? Ask God to give you courage to embrace humility, knowing that He will lift you up again.

Seeing God Through The Storm

Chapter 29

Grace

It's difficult to imagine myself in Job's place as God finished speaking to him. I'd probably have been facedown on the ground. God's revelation of Himself was so powerful it would have left me speechless. That's why I love Job's reply to God. Of all the things Job could have said, or all the things I might have said, Job's words are exactly what all of us need to hear.

> *Then Job replied to the LORD: "I know that you can do all things; no plan of yours can be thwarted. You asked, 'Who is this that obscures my counsel without knowledge?' Surely I spoke of things I did not understand, things too wonderful for me to know. You said, 'Listen now, and I will speak; I will question you, and you shall answer me.' My ears had heard of you but now my eyes have seen you. Therefore I despise myself and repent in dust and ashes."*
>
> -Job 42:1-6

No longer did Job complain about his circumstances or ask God for explanations. All words had been stilled by one emphatic statement—"I AM God!" Job acknowledged that God can do whatever He chooses. Job admitted there were things far beyond his limited knowledge, and he was ready to trust those things to God.

Before his suffering, Job had only "heard" of God. Now he had "seen" God.

Job's understanding of God was expanded so dramatically that his view of himself was altered. Instead of defending his blamelessness, Job repented *in dust and ashes*. In light of God's perfection, Job saw what a sinner he was. Compared to God's greatness, Job recognized his own smallness. Job trembled before the awesomeness of God, and it changed him.

Maybe, like me, you've read this part of Job's story and thought, "That's not fair! God allowed Job's troubles. He never gave Job any answers but instead questioned him. Then Job ended up sitting in dust and ashes."

Many times I've felt like something in this passage didn't make sense. Where was God's mercy, kindness, and grace? Then the Lord showed me a life-changing truth: God does not overwhelm us with His majesty and glory to frighten us away from Him but to prepare us to receive His grace.

Let's repeat that.

God does not overwhelm us with His majesty and glory to frighten us away from Him but to **prepare** us to **receive** His **grace**.

We see examples of this truth all through Scripture. Consider Isaiah's encounter with God.

> *In the year that King Uzziah died, I saw the Lord seated on a throne, high and exalted, and the train of His robe filled the temple. Above Him were seraphs, each with six wings...And they were calling to one another:*
>
> *"Holy, holy, holy is the LORD Almighty; the whole earth is full of His glory." At the sound of their voices the doorposts and thresholds shook and the temple was filled with smoke.*
>
> *"Woe to me!" I cried. "I am ruined! For I am a man of unclean lips, and I live among a people of unclean lips, and my eyes have seen the King, the LORD Almighty."*
>
> *Then one of the seraphs flew to me with a live coal in his hand, which he had taken with tongs from the altar. With it he touched my mouth and said, "See, this has touched your lips; your guilt is taken away and your sin atoned for." Then I heard the voice of the Lord saying, "Whom shall I send? And who will go for us?" And I said, "Here am I. Send me!"*
>
> -Isaiah 6:1-8

Seeing God Through The Storm

When Isaiah saw this vision of God, he cried out in fear and despair because he realized how sinful he was. Yet God was ready with an offering of grace and a mission for Isaiah. The Apostle John wrote about a similar experience.

> *I, John…was in the Spirit, and I heard behind me a loud voice like a trumpet… And when I turned I saw…someone "like a son of man," dressed in a robe reaching down to His feet and with a golden sash around His chest. His head and hair were white like wool, as white as snow, and His eyes were like blazing fire. His feet were like bronze glowing in a furnace, and His voice was like the sound of rushing waters. In His right hand he held seven stars, and out of his mouth came a sharp double-edged sword. His face was like the sun shining in all its brilliance.*
>
> *When I saw Him, I fell at His feet as though dead. Then He placed His right hand on me and said: "Do not be afraid. I am the First and the Last. I am the Living One; I was dead, and behold I am alive for ever…*
>
> *Write, therefore, what you have seen, what is now and what will take place later."*
> -Revelation 1:9-19

This glorious revelation of Jesus left John near death. Jesus touched John and spoke those beautiful words of grace, *Do not be afraid*. Then the Lord told John to record what he saw.

Isaiah, John, and many others in the Bible were first overwhelmed by God's majesty. Then they received sweet grace.

When we catch even a glimpse of the awesomeness of God, we will be afraid. We'll see the ugliness of our sin exposed. There's no other response to the revelation of God's glory. But God is not trying to scare us away. On the contrary, He's preparing us to come closer to Him as we receive His grace.

Grace is the kindness and favor of God that we could never deserve. The more we realize how undeserving we are, the more precious God's grace becomes to us.

Job was deeply humbled by his encounter with God. It was painful and frightening. But it prepared him to experience God's grace in a way he never had before. Notice what happened after Job's humbling before God.

> *The LORD blessed the latter part of Job's life more than the first. He had fourteen thousand sheep, six thousand camels, a thousand yoke of oxen and a thousand donkeys. And he also had seven sons and three daughters.*
>
> -Job 42:12-13

Before his trial, Job hadn't earned all his material blessings by living blamelessly. They were a gift of God's grace. After his trial, Job received more blessings, again through grace. Likewise, we cannot earn God's favor or blessings. John 1:16 says, *From the fullness of His grace we have all received one blessing after another.* Every blessing in our lives comes from God's grace to us in Jesus Christ.

The LORD takes us through storms so He can reveal more of Himself to us. As we understand more of who God is, we'll see ourselves with greater humility. And we'll learn to embrace His grace more and more in our lives.

In the middle of my health trial, my physical suffering reached an extreme level. For three weeks I lived on Benadryl, just trying to keep breathing and hold onto the last bit of sanity I had. I struggled day after day to keep trusting God. Finally, I gave up. I was overwhelmed by what felt like God's power and harshness in my life. I couldn't hold on to Him any longer. I couldn't even pray. I had nothing left to offer. In my eyes, my faith failed.

Not long after that awful moment, I heard the Lord whisper to my heart, "Your faith may fail, but my grace never fails."

> *"Your faith may fail, but my grace never fails"*

Oh, the power of the grace of God! He never let go of me. He forgave my unbelief. He renewed my faith and strengthened my heart—not because of anything I had done, but because of His grace.

I believe there is nothing on this earth as extraordinary as experiencing the grace of God. To see how awesome the LORD is and to receive more of His undeserved favor is worth the pain of any storm. And as we embrace more of God's grace, we move from only "hearing" about Him to "seeing" Him.

After his trial I imagine that Job viewed all of life in the light of God's grace. I'm sure he even thanked God for his ordeal because of the grace he experienced at the end.

However you feel in your storm right now, take heart. As you see the light of dawn after each night of darkness, you will see the grace of God after the storm.

Thinking It Through:

a) Have you ever been through a time when you felt like your faith failed? How do think God used that experience to prepare your heart to receive more of His grace?

b) What does the grace of God mean to you? Talk to God about what you've learned. Thank Him for His grace that never fails.

Seeing God Through The Storm

Chapter 30

Restoration

Job's encounter with God left him humbled and gave him a new understanding of the grace of God. But that isn't the end of his story.

> *After the LORD had said these things to Job, he said to Eliphaz the Temanite, "I am angry with you and your two friends, because you have not spoken of me what is right, as my servant Job has."*
>
> -Job 42:7

I love the fact that after Job humbled himself before the LORD, God reaffirmed him—in front of Job's friends. God said Job had spoken what was right of Him; He called Job his servant. Yes, God had rebuked Job, but He never rejected Job. And He had a plan for restoring Job.

God continued speaking to Eliphaz.

> *"So now take seven bulls and seven rams and go to my servant Job and sacrifice a burnt offering for yourselves. My servant Job will pray for you, and I will accept his prayer and not deal with you according to your folly. You have not spoken of me what is right, as my servant Job has." So Eliphaz the Temanite, Bildad the Shuhite and Zophar the Naamathite did what the LORD told them; and the LORD accepted Job's prayer.*
>
> -Job 42:8-9

God wanted Job to pray for his friends—to forgive them and extend to them the grace he had just experienced. His friends didn't deserve to be forgiven. Perhaps Job realized how much his friends needed to see God's grace displayed, but I imagine it wasn't an easy thing to forgive them. However, it was a necessary part of Job's own restoration, and he obeyed.

Once Job knew God had accepted his prayer, I believe his heart and soul were restored. For a long time he had cried for relief from his suffering, for a return to normal life. In the end God gave Job what he needed most—inner transformation.

In His grace God also restored Job's circumstances, not just to what they had been before, but even more.

> *After Job had prayed for his friends, the LORD made him prosperous again and gave him twice as much as he had before. All his brothers and sisters and everyone who had known him before came and ate with him in his house. They comforted and consoled him over all the trouble the LORD had brought upon him, and each one gave him a piece of silver and a gold ring.*
>
> *The LORD blessed the latter part of Job's life more than the first. He had fourteen thousand sheep, six thousand camels, a thousand yoke of oxen and a thousand donkeys. And he also had seven sons and three daughters.*
>
> -Job 42:10-13

When we read this passage, it's easy to miss the fact that though Job was immediately restored spiritually, the restoration of his circumstances took time. Remember, he had nothing. He had to start over, using the gifts of his friends and relatives to purchase animals, supplies, etc. Even with God's blessing, it surely took Job years of hard work and dedication to rebuild his flocks and herds, not to mention having ten more children.

Many times restoration is a process. And spiritual and physical restoration don't always happen at the same time.

Five and a half years into my health trial, I had learned a lot. I had received much inner healing and even made tiny steps of progress in my health. Then the pressure of my circumstances once again made me to cry out to God for answers. The Lord revealed something I never expected. He showed me a lie I'd believed since age fourteen that had kept my spirit in bondage ever since.

A traumatic experience had caused me to believe there was something inherently wrong with me. Because I was deceived, I didn't consciously realize how much this lie affected every area of my life. When God opened my eyes to see it, I was able to receive His healing truth—I am fearfully and wonderfully made (Ps. 139:14). I am perfect and complete in Christ (Col. 2:10). It was a beautiful moment of freedom for me!

Then God reminded me that I needed to forgive the person whose actions caused me to believe the lie. For years I thought I had forgiven, but I didn't realize how deeply I'd been wounded. Forgiving that person completely was one of the hardest things I've ever done. But it wasn't until I forgave that God graciously bought back to life that part of me that died at age fourteen.

Through the anguish and agony of my storm, the LORD beautifully restored my soul. I felt like a new person, like the "me" I was created to be. I was literally ready to take on the world!

Yet, while my spirit was bursting with new vitality, my body was still weak and sick. My spiritual restoration happened in that moment, but my physical restoration has been a slow process that continues three years later. I praise God that He has restored many physical blessings to me over the last few years—including being able to go to church again. Only God knows when my health will be fully restored. Until then I rejoice in the process of restoration He is working out in my life.

the Lord loves to restore our souls

While I can't promise the restoration of specific circumstances, I can assure you that the Lord loves to restore our souls. Perhaps, as He did with me, He's allowed your storm so He can bring restoration to your heart. Maybe you've been focused on wanting your circumstances restored. Many times God does restore them. We can always ask Him to return lost health, relationships, finances, etc., and we can know He'll do what's best for us. But clearly God's priority is our hearts. Circumstances constantly change, but our relationship with God will last for eternity.

If I had to choose, I would gladly choose my spiritual restoration regardless of what circumstances came with it. I'm sure Job would say the same thing. Yes, his health and prosperity were restored to him, but undoubtedly it was not Job's possessions, but his restored soul that kept the glow of joy continually burning in his heart.

Thinking It Through:

a) Have you been praying for a long time for God to restore your circumstances? How has this chapter encouraged you to keep trusting Him to work out His perfect plan for you?

b) Are you in need of spiritual restoration in any area today? Spend some time in prayer—asking, listening, and waiting on the Lord. Let Him guide you; He is your Shepherd who restores your soul (Ps. 23:1-3).

Seeing God Through The Storm

Chapter 31

Legacy

Here we are at the end of the book of Job. Have you found comfort and encouragement from Job's story? I have. I'd never wish such intense suffering on anyone, but I'm grateful God gave us this record of Job's experience. Because of what he went through, we've learned many precious truths about how to see God in our storms.

We've discovered that the LORD is in control, He is good, and He has a purpose for us. We've found that we don't have to be afraid, that God's love surrounds us, and that His wisdom is perfect. We've come to know God as the Healer of our hearts, the Repairer of our broken pieces, and the Restorer of our souls. Above all, we've begun to understand that our holy God is gracious beyond measure.

In His grace, God didn't just restore Job. God also gave Job a valuable legacy from his suffering. Not only was Job's life changed, but his friends' lives were changed. All who knew Job were surely impacted as well.

After this, Job lived a hundred and forty years; he saw his children and their children to the fourth generation. And so he died, old and full of years.

-Job 42:16-17

I imagine that Job never stopped telling his grandchildren and great-grandchildren the story of his encounter with God and how it radically altered his life. Now you and I have been affected by his story, too. Undoubtedly Job had no idea of the far-reaching impact his trial would have. But God knew. The Lord allowed Job's storm both to transform Job's life and to bless others.

It's significant that nowhere in the final chapter of Job is Satan mentioned. Isn't he the one who started all the trouble? Yet at the end of the story, he's conspicuously absent. I believe that's because this story is not about Satan at all. It's about GOD. It's about what God wanted to do in Job's life. It's about the millions of people God wanted to touch through Job's suffering.

Yes, Satan is real, and he's always trying to destroy God's people. At times we may feel overwhelmed by his attacks, but we can have confidence that our trials are not really about Satan's activity. Our storms are about what God wants to accomplish in us and through us for His glory.

What a beautiful gift it is to know that God has a legacy planned for our trials! A legacy is something that endures, something meaningful that is passed along to others, something precious that remains after the storm and even after we are gone. Can you imagine that God wants to use your suffering to bless other people?

> **God wants to use your suffering to bless other people**

Many times we may feel like we have nothing we can give, nothing we can use to bless others. But we always have grace. After Job's encounter with God, he was a changed man—on the inside. Externally though, his hands were empty. When God told Job to pray for his friends, He didn't ask Job to provide the animals for the sacrifices. Job didn't have any. Job had only one thing to give, the most precious thing God had given him—grace.

Just as God continually floods us with His abundant grace, He will also empower us to give grace away to others.

And God is able to make all grace abound to you, so that in all things at all times, having all that you need, you will abound in every good work.
-2 Corinthians 9:8

Storms may take our resources, our health, even our relationships, but they cannot take from us the super-abundant grace of God! In light of eternity, the best gift we can give anyone is the gift of grace. We can give grace through forgiveness, prayer, encouraging words, acts of kindness, even a smile. When we extend grace to others, though it seems small, it will eventually have an impact far beyond what we can see now.

I could write a long list of the ways God has used my health trial for His glory. Through my storm, God has encouraged many of my friends. He has blessed people I've never met and led at least one person to saving faith in Jesus. Also, if I hadn't experienced the suffering of the last eight and a half years, I never would have written this book.

God has used my storm not only to heal, transform, and restore me, but also to impact many other lives. And my trial isn't over! I can't wait to see what other wonderful blessings God will bring from it.

The legacy God wants to give you from your storm may not be at all what you expect. It may be huge, beyond anything you could imagine (Eph. 3:20). Or it may seem so small that you don't immediately recognize it. In His perfect way and time, the LORD will reveal His legacy for you.

Job's marathon trial was finally over. He had experienced horrible suffering, but in the end he saw God in his storm. And his story continues to bless people thousands of years later. Though our trials may not seem as huge or as significant as Job's, we know God has a purpose for every storm we go through, large or small.

Like Job, we too can leave a legacy for others. Each storm is an opportunity for us to get to know God better—to "see" Him instead of only "hearing" of Him. As our understanding of God's character and grace expands, our intimacy with Him will deepen. And He will work through us to share His truth and show His grace to others.

As we continue on life's journey, I pray we'll learn to see our gracious God in each storm and trust Him to bring about the beautiful legacy He has planned for us.

...No eye has seen, no ear has heard, no mind has conceived what God has prepared for those who love Him—
-1 Corinthians 2:9

> **Thinking It Through:**

a) How does understanding more of God's grace toward you change your attitude toward others?

b) Do you believe God can use your trial to bless other people? Ask God to show you the opportunities He has planned for you—opportunities to share what you've learned and to extend grace to others. Whether you can see it yet or not, praise the LORD for the legacy He will give you from your storm.

God Of The Storm

Lightning, thunder, wind,
A raging storm rolls in.
My calm life fades, questions reign.
God of the thunder, help me hear you.
Your power astounds me,
I acknowledge your mighty name.

In pain and suffering,
In doubt and wondering,
Only you have the answers I need.
God of the darkness, help me trust you.
Your wisdom confounds me,
I confess your holy name.

In trouble, teaching,
In weakness, strengthening,
You never leave me, my Savior.
God of the rain, help me rest in you.
Your love surrounds me,
I worship your faithful name.

Though the journey's long,
By faith I press on,
Watching broken become beautiful.
God of the storm, help me see you.
Your grace abounds to me,
I bless your name, my LORD.

Seeing God Through The Storm

Final Thoughts

Thank you so much for journeying with me through the book of Job! After all the time, energy, prayers, and tears I've poured into this project, it's hard to say goodbye.

It's taken me more than three years to write this book, and it went through more revisions than anything else I've written. Perhaps I should have expected a difficult path considering the topic. I never would have attempted it, except I knew this was God's assignment for me. I've learned so much through the process, and I praise God for His power and grace that has brought it to completion.

I pray that the truths in this book have touched your life as deeply as they have touched mine. I pray you will continue to experience God's transforming work in your life. I praise God for you and for what He will do in and through you.

I'd love to hear from you! Let me know what God is doing in your life or how I can pray for you. You can e-mail me at Joanna@Godisgracious.net or stop by my website: http://godisgracious.net/

I look forward to an eternity of swapping stories of the power and grace of our awesome God! For now, may you see Him more in every storm until you see Him face to face in glory.

Your sister on the journey,

-Joanna

Discussion Guide

The following questions are provided to facilitate discussion for small groups, Sunday School classes, one-on-one mentoring, etc.

Begin each meeting with prayer, asking the Lord to grant understanding, to open hearts and minds, and to bring transformation through His truth.

Please note that the "Thinking It Through" questions from the end of each chapter are included in the list of discussion questions. So, after reading the chapter, you can proceed straight to the questions here in the Discussion Guide.

Chapter 1 – *Pleasing To God*

1) On a scale of one to ten, how hard is it for you to embrace the truth that you are pleasing to God? Discuss what thoughts or attitudes might keep you from believing God is pleased with you.

2) Read Matthew 3:16-17. How does God the Father view Jesus?

3) Read Ephesians 1:3-14. How many times does the passage say *in Christ* or *in Him*? List all the benefits we have in Christ according to these verses.

4) What does it mean to you that you are in Christ?

5) What do you think is the reason for your current storm? What can you do to help you see your trial as a blessing from God?

6) Read Question a) from the "Thinking It Through" questions at the end of Chapter 1. Share about your salvation experience with the person next to you, or discuss any questions you have about salvation. Then say to each other, "You are pleasing to God in Christ!"

7) Read Question b) from the "Thinking It Through" questions at the end of Chapter 1. Praise God together that He is pleased with you because of Jesus.

Chapter 2 – *The LORD*

1) What is your usual response to the trials in your life? How do you think you would have responded in Job's situation?

2) Do you ever feel like you're at the mercy of Satan, wicked people, or your own mistakes? Describe your view of who or what is in control both of the world and of your circumstances.

3) Read Isaiah 45:6-7 and Psalm 103:19. List some reasons why it's hard to believe God is in control of all things.

4) Discuss your answer to Question a) from the "Thinking It Through" questions at the end of Chapter 2.

5) In what situations in your life do you need to acknowledge God's sovereignty?

6) Read Psalm 9:10. How can knowing the name of the LORD help you to trust Him?

7) Read Question b) from the "Thinking It Through" questions. Take time to bless the name of the LORD. Pray for each other to be able to praise God in the storm.

Chapter 3 – *Not My God*

1) Why is it that none of us knows God as well as we think we do?

2) Discuss Question a) from the end of Chapter 3.

3) Read Deuteronomy 29:29, 1 Timothy 6:15-16, and Psalm 14:2. What do you think about the paradox that we cannot completely understand God, yet He wants us to know Him better?

4) Share about a time when God caused you to question what you thought you knew about Him in order to help you discover the truth you needed to know about Him.

5) What unexplained hardships are trying to push you away from God? How can you seek Him instead?

6) Share your answers to Question b) from the end of the chapter.

7) Read Jeremiah 9:23-24. What do you think is God's desire for you in your current storm? Spend a few minutes in prayer, asking God to reveal more of Himself through your trials.

Chapter 4 – *No Wrong*

1) Describe how you felt during a time when your difficult circumstances went from bad to worse.

2) What arguments do people often use to claim that God is not good? By what standard do you measure God's goodness?

3) How do you define the goodness of God? Read Deuteronomy 32:4 and Psalm 18:30, and discuss what you think is a biblical definition of God's goodness.

4) Share your answers to Question a) from the chapter.

5) Read 2 Corinthians 5:7. Are you ready to take a step of faith by choosing to believe that God is good?

6) Discuss Question b) from the chapter.

7) Read out loud Psalm 100:5, Psalm 118:1, and John 10:14. Praise God for His goodness, and pray for one another to be strengthened in your belief that God is indeed good.

Chapter 5 – *Perspective*

1) What difficulties tend to distort your perspective?

2) In comparison to Job's trial how bad is your storm?

3) Share your answer to Question a) from the chapter with the person next to you.

4) Read 1 Thessalonians 5:18 and Psalm 50:23. How does giving thanks help us view things from God's perspective?

5) Read Psalm 5:12. Even if, like Job, you had nothing, what does it mean to you that you always have God's favor in Jesus?

6) Read 2 Corinthians 10:7a. Have you been looking only on the surface of your trial? What deeper perspective might God want you to see?

7) Discuss Question b) from the chapter. Pray for any specific situations in which you're struggling to keep God's perspective.

Chapter 6 – *Purpose*

1) Share about a time when you questioned the value of your existence.

2) Why is it hard to remember that your life has purpose?

3) What kinds of heart response to God bring Him glory?

4) When you read Ephesians 2:10, what type of *good works* immediately come to mind? Do you think your concept of *good works* has been too limited? If so, in what way?

5) Do you believe it's possible for your storm to stop God's plan for you? Why or why not? Can you accept that your trial may be necessary to fulfill God's purpose for you?

6) Share your answers to Question a) from the chapter.

7) Discuss Question b) from the chapter. Read Isaiah 14:24. Spend time praising God that He has a purpose for your life and for your storm.

Chapter 7 – *No Fear*

1) Discuss Question a) from the chapter.

2) Why is living with fear often more harmful than our stressful situations?

3) What do you usually do to combat fear in your life? How well is it working? Based on the verses in this chapter, what might you do differently?

4) How do you define the love of God? Read Ephesians 3:17b-19. How often do you think about and consider God's love for you?

5) Read Psalm 112:7-8. Why is it possible for us to have no fear, even in the face of bad news or difficult circumstances?

6) Do you believe that everything God allows in your life is motivated by His love for you? Why or why not? Read Psalm 145:13b, 17.

7) Read Question b) from the chapter and share your thoughts. Spend time praying for one another.

Chapter 8 – *Open Heart*

1) Discuss Question a) from the chapter.

2) Do you believe God can use even painful comments for good in your life? Share about a time when you heard something worthwhile in a person's unwelcome words.

3) Read Psalm 131:1a. How can we learn to swallow our pride and acknowledge any truth in someone's unkind words?

4) Discuss how can we release resentment and move toward having an open heart. Read James 4:6.

5) How often do you think about God's forgiveness and grace toward you? When you consider these gifts, what is your response? Read Psalm 130:3-4.

6) Describe someone you know who you think has an open heart. What do you admire most about them?

7) Answer Question b) from the chapter. Spend a few minutes praying for one another.

Chapter 9 – *Heal Me*

1) Have you been afraid to let God expose your inner needs? Why do you think He wants to reveal them to you?

2) Read Question a) from the chapter. Do you know anyone who doesn't need healing in their spirit? Why do you think we often resist the process of inner healing?

3) Read Proverbs 14:30 and Ephesians 4:26-27. Why is giving and receiving forgiveness vital to inner healing?

4) How often do negative comments from other people replay in your mind? What specific verses can help you replace those thoughts with God's thoughts? Read Psalm 139:17-18.

5) Share any ways you have experienced God's supernatural healing touch in your spirit. How did this healing change you?

6) Why do you think inner healing is a life-long process? What does it mean to you that God wants you to know Him as your Healer?

7) Read Question b) from the chapter. Pray for one another to experience God's healing work day by day.

Chapter 10 – *No More*

1) What *impetuous* words have you spoken to God in your storm?

2) Discuss Job's prayer in Job 6:8-10. What do you think about his motivation and his request? Have you ever felt or prayed something similar?

3) Read Question a) from the chapter. Share your experience. If you haven't experienced this, how can you be better prepared for such a moment?

4) Read 2 Corinthians 1:8-10. When your storm is beyond your ability to endure, what can you do? What can God do for you?

5) Share your answer to Question b) from the chapter.

6) Read the poem at the end of the chapter. Do you believe God is enough for your need—and even more? Turn to the person next to you and say, "God is enough for you!"

7) Read Psalm 73:26. Praise God that He is more than enough to carry you through your storm.

Chapter 11 – *Forgiven*

1) Read Colossians 2:13-14. What is the basis of God's forgiveness for us? How many of our sins were forgiven at the cross?

2) Read Psalm 103:12, Isaiah 1:18, 43:25, and 44:22. When God forgives, what does He do with your sin? How does that make you feel?

3) How have you pictured God's attitude of forgiveness toward you? Does your perspective need an adjustment?

4) Share your answer to Question a) from the chapter.

5) Are you carrying guilt or regret for a sin that God has forgiven? What can you do to lay down that burden?

6) Is there anyone you need to forgive today? How can thinking about God's awesome forgiveness toward you help you to forgive that person? Read Ephesians 4:32.

7) Read Question b) from the chapter. Spend a few minutes in silent prayer. Then praise God together for His wonderful gift of forgiveness!

Chapter 12 – *God-Centered*

1) When someone asks, "Why do bad things happen to good people?" what is your usual response?

2) Do you know anyone who agrees with Bildad's formula for life? ("If you sin, you'll suffer; if you're righteous, you'll prosper.") How would you describe that person?

3) Read Romans 3:23-24. Is it difficult for you to admit that you're not a good person? Why or why not?

4) List some of the good things God has given you in Christ.

5) Why is it hard to see our bad circumstances as something God can use for good? Share your answer to Question a) from the chapter.

6) Read Psalm 119:15-16. How can we develop a more God-centered focus?

7) Discuss Question b) from the chapter. Praise God for His gift of grace, and pray for each other to grow in a God-centered perspective.

Chapter 13 – *Surrounded*

1) Why does the knowledge of God's power give us little comfort without the assurance of His love?

2) Share your answer to Question a) from the chapter.

3) List some reasons we may not feel like God loves us. What do all these reasons reveal about our view of God?

4) Read John 17:25-26. What do we need in order to expand our concept of God's love? How can storms deepen our understanding of God?

5) Read 1 John 4:8-10 and Psalm 145:17. Why does God love us? Based on what God has said about Himself in the Bible, is it possible for Him not to love you?

6) Think about the past week. What expressions of love did God send you? How can you learn to be more aware of His displays of love for you?

7) Share your answer to Question b) from the chapter. Spend some time in prayer together.

Chapter 14 – *God's Heart*

1) Discuss Question a) from the chapter.
2) How can having a wrong opinion about God pull you away from Him?
3) Which truths about God do you sometimes doubt are true in your own life? What do you think causes the disconnect from what you know is true to actually believing it for your specific situation?
4) Read Hosea 4:6a, 2 Corinthians 10:5, and 2 Peter 1:2-3. List all the reasons from these verses why it's important for us to know God's heart.
5) Do you believe that God wants you to know Him? What is the biggest obstacle in your life to knowing God better?
6) Discuss ideas of specific actions you can take this week to know God better through His Word and through focusing on Jesus.
7) Share your answers to Question b) from the chapter. Pray for each other to keep learning to trust God's heart.

Chapter 15 – *Unlimited*

1) Why is it sometimes hard to remember that our storms have a limit, that they won't last forever?
2) Discuss your answers to Question a) from the chapter.
3) Read Psalm 36:5-7 and list the unlimited attributes of God that are mentioned. How does understanding God's unlimited character help us take refuge in Him?
4) When you consider that God has no limits, what is your response? How could meditating on this truth each day change the way you live?
5) Share about a time when you were amazed by something wonderful in creation. Do you feel that same sense of awe when thinking about who God is?
6) Read 2 Corinthians 9:8. Do you sometimes think of God's grace toward you as limited? What does it mean to you that not only God's character is unlimited, but His supply of grace is unlimited?
7) Read Question b) from the chapter. Take turns praising God for your favorite attribute of His character. Or, sing a praise song together, worshiping the LORD.

Chapter 16 – *God's Wisdom*

1) Read and discuss Question a) from the chapter.

2) What are some of the results of relying on our own understanding?

3) Why is it sometimes difficult to trust God's wisdom in our circumstances? What specific thoughts or attitudes often keep you from trusting God's wisdom?

4) Read the following verses and discuss how we develop true godly wisdom: Psalm 111:10, Proverbs 2:6, 11:2, 13:20, and Romans 12:1-2.

5) How can trusting God's wisdom in our lives be a testimony to those around us? Read Psalm 119:74 and Philippians 1:12-14.

6) What things can we do to stay motivated to trust God's wisdom on a daily basis?

7) Read Question b) from the chapter and share your thoughts. Spend time praying for one another.

Chapter 17 – *Intimacy*

1) What or who do you long for most in life? Discuss how much greater you think God's longing is for you.

2) Share your answers to Question a) from the chapter.

3) Why is it hard to accept that suffering is God's invitation for us to draw closer to Him? Read and discuss 1 Peter 4:12-13.

4) Share some examples of how you've gotten to know Jesus better in a time of suffering.

5) What things often hinder you from responding to God's loving pursuit?

6) Read Psalm 73:16-17, 23-26, 28. What are some benefits of turning to God even when you don't feel like it?

7) Discuss Question b) from the chapter. Pray for each other to grow in intimacy with Jesus.

Chapter 18 – *For Me*

1) Share about a time when someone demonstrated that they were "for you." How did their actions affect you?

2) Have you ever felt like God was against you? How did it affect your relationship with Him?

3) Why does Satan want us to think God is against us?

4) Read Romans 5:1-2 and Hebrews 4:14-16, then discuss Question a) from the chapter.

5) What is your response when you consider that Jesus is praying for you?

6) Read Psalm 118:6-7 and Hebrews 13:6. If you're facing a difficult situation right now, how can knowing God is for you help you?

7) Read Question b) from the chapter. Encourage one another by sharing some ways that God has shown His care for you recently. Turn to the person next to you and say, "God is for you!" End with a time of praise to our gracious God.

Chapter 19 – *True Justice*

1) Who have you been tempted to envy lately? Do you think this envy comes from questioning God's justice about something? Explain.

2) Why is it hard for us to wait until eternity to see God's complete justice?

3) Discuss Question a) from the chapter.

4) David understood about waiting for God's justice. Read Psalm 35:17-18. How can we focus on God's eternal character instead of on our immediate circumstances?

5) Read 1 Timothy 1:12-14. How does experiencing God's grace change our view of His justice?

6) Would you change God's timing for justice if you could? Why or why not? How can understanding His true justice give you a sense of security today?

7) Read Question b) from the chapter and share your thoughts. Pray for each other to be encouraged and to find rest in God's perfect, eternal character.

Chapter 20 – *Brokenness*

1) How would you define brokenness?

2) Share your answers to Question a) from the chapter.

3) What obstacles might be keeping you from total surrender to God?

4) Why must self be dethroned before Jesus can live through us? Read Romans 7:18a and John 15:4-5.

5) Do you agree that brokenness is not a punishment but a preparation? Why is brokenness the path to fruitfulness? Read God's words to Israel in Hosea 14:8b.

6) Read the poem from the end of the chapter. Is it difficult for you to believe God can change your brokenness into something beautiful? Why or why not?

7) Read Question b) from the chapter and take a few minutes to write your lists. Then spend time praying for each other and praising God by faith for what He will do!

Chapter 21 – *Hope*

1) Read Psalm 71:5 again. How is biblical hope different from the way we commonly use the word hope today? Discuss Question a) from the chapter.

2) Why can we hope in God regardless of our circumstances?

3) Explain the process God often uses to build hope in our lives (from Rom. 5:2-5). How have you seen this process at work in your own life?

4) In Isaiah 49:23c, God said, *Then you will know that I am the LORD; those who hope in me will not be disappointed.* Take a moment and consider—do you think it's possible to have the kind of hope that will never be disappointed? Why or why not?

5) Read Romans 15:13. Who empowers us to live in hope? How does this truth encourage you?

6) Share your answers to Question b) from the chapter.

7) Break into pairs and share about any areas where you're struggling to keep your hope in God. Pray for each other to be strengthened in and overflow with hope this week.

Chapter 22 – *Faith*

1) What has been your definition of faith up to this point? What do you think about the statement that faith is "agreeing with an invisible reality"?

2) List some truths that you are absolutely sure and certain about (List A). Now list some things you know intellectually are true but sometimes find difficult to believe (List B). What do you think causes certain truths to move from head knowledge (List B) to a certainty in your soul (List A)?

3) What role do trials play in growing our faith? Read James 1:2-4.

4) Discuss Question a) from the chapter

5) Why do you think God values faith more than men value gold?

6) Though learning to "see" what is unseen does not come naturally, what are some of the benefits of practicing faith? Read Isaiah 26:3 and 1 Peter 1:8, then share any other verses you can think of that answer this question.

7) Read 2 Corinthians 4:18 again and discuss Question b) from the chapter. Spend some time praising God for His faithfulness.

Chapter 23 – *Glory And Honor*

1) What has been your primary goal in your storm? What goal do you think God wants you to have?

2) Discuss Question a) from the chapter. Why does the way we live matter to God? Read 1 Peter 4:11.

3) What are some ways you've tried to honor God in your own strength in the past? What were the results of your efforts?

4) Share about a time when God worked through your weakness to display His strength. What results did you see then?

5) Read Galatians 2:20 and Matthew 11:28-29. Discuss how these verses encourage you to rest in Christ's life in you.

6) How has this chapter changed your thinking about what it means to honor God?

7) Read Question b) from the chapter, and pray together as the Lord leads you.

Chapter 24 – *Most Valuable*

1) Share your answers to Question a) from the chapter.

2) What sometimes hinders you from seeing God as the most valuable One in your life?

3) Read Psalm 63:1-5. Why could David praise God in a barren place?

4) Discuss the differences between enjoying God's gifts and enjoying Him.

5) Share about a time when God withdrew some of His gifts in order to draw you closer to Himself.

6) What are some ways we can practice delighting in the Lord? Read Mark 6:31, Colossians 3:16 and Psalm 68:3-4 to start your discussion.

7) Discuss Question b) from the chapter. Spend a few minutes praying for each other.

Chapter 25 – *Motivation*

1) How often do you think about why you do what you do—is it all the time or not at all? Discuss what you consider a healthy approach to monitoring your motivation. Read Psalm 139:23-24.

2) Share you answers to Question a) from the chapter.

3) Why do you think God wants to transform our motivation for following Him from fear to love? Share any verses you can think of that apply.

4) How can you learn to recognize when you're being driven by fear or led by love? Read Romans 8:14-16.

5) Do you think love is the most powerful motivation there is? Why or why not?

6) If our motive for following Jesus is love, how might that affect our motivation in other areas of life? Read Philippians 1:9-11.

7) Share your thoughts about Question b) from the chapter. Praise God together for how He is working in your lives and for what He will continue to do.

Chapter 26 – *God Speaks*

1) Have you experienced a time when it seemed like God was silent? How did you respond?
2) Discuss Question a) from the chapter.
3) List some habits we can develop that will help us learn to hear God speak. To get started, read Psalm 37:7a, Psalm 119:11, and Proverbs 3:5-6.
4) How can we know that something we "hear" is indeed God speaking to us?
5) Share your answers to Question b) from the chapter.
6) What have you learned about the ongoing process of perceiving God's voice? Share some verses that comfort you during times when it seems like God is silent.
7) Spend some time in silence, practicing a quiet, listening heart—whether you hear anything or not.

Chapter 27 – *Look Around*

1) Why do you think God's first words to Job after His silence were questions, not answers?
2) How often do you spend time out in creation observing and enjoying it? What have you learned about God from those times?
3) How can the practice of seeing God in creation help our perspective, especially during trials? Read Psalm 121:1-2.
4) Discuss Question a) from the chapter.
5) Select an attribute of God mentioned in this chapter and discuss how you can apply it to your current storm.
6) Do you agree that knowing God as "I AM" is the only answer we truly need? Why or why not? Read Psalm 46:10.
7) Read Question b) from the chapter. Pray for each other to be encouraged as you see more of God in His creation this week.

Chapter 28 – *Tremble*

1) Discuss Question a) from the chapter.
2) If you'd been in Job's place, how might you have felt or responded after God spoke?
3) Read Matthew 23:12 and Philippians 2:5-11. Why do you think God esteems those who are humble and tremble before Him?
4) Share about a difficult, humbling experience that you were later grateful for.
5) What are some benefits of humility you can recall when you're tempted to resist a humbling moment? Read Proverbs 11:2, Proverbs 18:12, and James 3:13.
6) Discuss the statement "Love always knows what we need." How have you seen this truth at work in your life?
7) Read Question b) from the chapter. Spend some time in silence, humbling yourself before the Lord. Then thank God for His promise to lift up those who humble themselves before Him.

Chapter 29 – *Grace*

1) What do you find significant about Job's reply to God in Job 42:1-6?
2) Share about a time when your view of God was expanded so much that it changed your view of yourself.
3) Discuss the statement: "God does not overwhelm us with His majesty and glory to frighten us away from Him but to prepare us to receive His grace." Name some biblical examples of this truth in addition to Isaiah and John.
4) Why does understanding God's majesty precede receiving more of His grace? What do you think is the connection between experiencing God's grace and seeing Him in your storm?
5) Read Lamentations 3:21-23. Share your answers to Question a) from the chapter.
6) Discuss Question b) from the chapter. What have you learned about God's grace from this chapter?
7) Read Isaiah 30:18. Praise God together for His unfailing grace.

Chapter 30 – *Restoration*

1) Obviously Job wasn't going to disobey God's command, but how do you think he felt as he prayed for his friends? What would you have been thinking in his place?

2) Why do you think forgiving others often plays a role in our spiritual restoration? Read Ephesians 4:26-27, 32.

3) In the past, have you expected spiritual and physical restoration to happen simultaneously? What benefits are there for us when they occur separately?

4) Discuss Question a) from the chapter. Read Jeremiah 29:11 and Psalm 31:14-15, 19.

5) Why do you think God is more focused on our spiritual condition than our physical state?

6) When you contemplate God's willingness and ability to restore us, what is your response?

7) Read Question b) from the chapter. Break into pairs and pray for each other, asking God to bring any needed restoration.

Chapter 31 – *Legacy*

1) Discuss the concept of a legacy. What is it? What is its value?

2) Share about someone you know who is living out a meaningful legacy following a painful trial.

3) Why do you think Satan is completely absent from the final chapters of Job? What significance does that fact have for our own trials? Read Romans 8:18 and 2 Corinthians 4:17.

4) What is your response to the truth that "we always have grace"? How have you seen God's grace displayed both to you and through you in your current storm?

5) Share your answer to Question a) from the chapter.

6) Read the poem from the end of the chapter. How has your perspective on storms changed? What new attitudes will you take with you into any new storms that come? Read Psalm 77:11-14 out loud together.

7) Read Question b) from the chapter. Encourage one another about the opportunities you see God providing. Spend time praising your gracious God for all He has done and all He will do in your lives!

Acknowledgements

This book was not only a challenge, it was a spiritual battle from beginning to end. I'd never have completed it without the help, support, and prayers of many wonderful people.

Reg Garner – Thank you for the incredible cover photo! It beautifully expresses the theme of this book. It was an answer to months of prayer, and I praise God for your talent and kindness.

Dr. Hawkins and **Cynthia Heald** – I'm humbled by and grateful for your encouragement, support and prayers. Thank you for taking the time to read this manuscript and to invest in my life. I praise God for your lives and the blessing you are to me.

My prayer supporters – You guys are awesome! Thank you for lifting me up and carrying me in your prayers. I'm so thankful for your partnership in this ministry. I couldn't do it without you!

My volunteer readers – Thank you for taking the time to share your thoughts. Your helpful and encouraging feedback made this book much richer.

Jenn Abbott – I can't imagine the last nine years without your friendship! Thank you for always listening, loving, encouraging, and praying for me, even in the midst of your own storms. I praise God for blessing me with a friend like you, who "sticks closer than a brother."

Howard & Bonnie Lisech – I thank God for your faithful love, encouragement and prayers. Thanks for being my shelter in the storm time and again. I love you both so much!

My family – Thank you for loving me and praying for me through my storm. If Job had had family like you, I imagine his might have been a different story. I praise God for blessing me with all of you!

Mom – As always, you went above and beyond to make this book what God wanted it to be. You've made me a better writer and a richer Christ-follower. Thank you for everything you do for me and for your daily example of seeing God in every storm. I love you muchisimo!

My gracious God – Words cannot express my gratitude or love for you. "Thank you" seems so small, but I offer it to you with all I am. Thank you for carrying me through my storm and for bringing me to a more beautiful place with you than I ever dreamed possible! You are my joy, my life, my all.

Other Books Available from Deeper Roots Publications

HE'S MY GOD! *Book 1* – JOANNA K. Harris & Jen Kallin
    Knowing God Through His Names – A Children's Devotional

HE'S MY GOD! *Book 2* – JOANNA K. Harris & Jen Kallin
    Knowing God Through His Names – A Children's Devotional

GRACE IN TIME OF NEED – JOANNA K. Harris
    Encouragement For Those Who Are Suffering

FRUIT THAT REMAINS – Bonnie Lisech
    Spiritual Growth Through Life Experience

ENCOURAGEMENT FOR HOME SCHOOL MOMS (BOOK 1) – Bonnie Lisech

ENCOURAGEMENT FOR HOME SCHOOL MOMS (BOOK 2) – Bonnie Lisech

PRE–FIELD PREPARATION - *7 and 14 day Editions* – Howard & Bonnie Lisech

WALK AS HE WALKED - *50 day, 30 day, 21 day, and 14 day Editions* – Howard & Bonnie Lisech

ABIDE IN THE VINE - *50 day, 21 day, and 14 day Editions* – Howard & Bonnie Lisech

RIPE FOR HARVEST - *21 day, and 14 day Editions* – Howard & Bonnie Lisech

LIVE IN THE LIGHT - *14 day Edition* – Howard & Bonnie Lisech

COMING HOME *Book 1* - *14 day Overseas Return Edition* – Howard & Bonnie Lisech
    Reentry Devotions for a Successful Return

COMING HOME AGAIN *Book 2* - *14 day Overseas Return Edition* – Howard & Bonnie Lisech
    Reentry Devotions for Another Successful Return

RETURNING HOME *Book 3* - *14 day Overseas Return Edition* – Howard & Bonnie Lisech
    Reentry Devotions for a Successful Return

REENTRY GUIDE FOR SHORT TERM MISSION LEADERS – Lisa Espinelli Chinn

BEFORE YOU GO – Howard Erickson
    A Short-Term Missions Manual

FIRM FOUNDATIONS: CREATION TO CHRIST (PARTS 1 & 2) – Jan L. Harris
    5-6th Grade Bible Curriculum

DISCOVERING OUR AMAZING GOD *Book 1* – Harris & Lisech
    7th Grade Bible Curriculum

DISCOVERING WHO I AM IN CHRIST *Book 2* – Harris & Lisech
    8th Grade Bible Curriculum

DISCOVERING CHRISTLIKE HABITS *Book 3* – Harris & Lisech
    9th Grade Bible Curriculum

DISCOVERING CHRISTLIKE CHARACTER *Book 4* – Harris & Lisech
    Can be used for 10th Grade Bible Curriculum

ROOTED & GROUNDED – A GUIDE FOR SPIRITUAL GROWTH
    10-12th Grade & Adult Bible Curriculum – Lisech & Harris